Flight from the City

*An Experiment in Creative Living on the Land –
Moving to the Country; Fresh Food, a Large Rural
Home, and a Relaxed, Happier Life*

By Ralph Borsodi

PANTIANOS
CLASSICS

Published by Pantianos Classics

ISBN-13: 978-1-78987-127-2

First published in 1933

Contents

Prelude to The First Edition

THIS book is written in response to hundreds of requests for some detailed description of the way of life and of the experiments with domestic production referred to in my previous book, *This Ugly Civilization.* Since the collapse of the great boom in October, 1929, these requests have greatly increased in number.

It is not an exaggeration of the situation today to say that millions of urban families are considering the possibility of flight from the city to the country. But the realization that there had been for fully half a century a flight of millions from the country to the city seems to me an essential prelude to consideration of any move back to the land. Not only had the *proportion* of farm population to city population in the United States declined over a long period of years, but for many years prior to 1930, the *total farm population* of the nation itself declined. Since 1930, and the ending of the last period of city "prosperity," the movement has completely reversed itself, as is shown by the table:

This migration of millions, back and forth, between city and country, is to me evidence of profound dissatisfaction with living conditions both in the country and in the city. It is something which those considering a change in their ways of living should carefully ponder. The industrialization of agriculture during the past century--its transformation from a way of life to a commercial business--has very clearly increased the migration of farmers and farm-bred people from

MOVEMENT OF POPULATION TO AND FROM FARMS

During year	Total farm population on January 1st of each year	Persons leaving farms for cities[3]	Persons arriving at farms from cities[3]	Net movement from farms to cities[3]
1910.......	32,976,960[1]	.....	.....	.....
1920.......	31,614,269[2]	896,000	560,000	336,000
1921.......	31,703,000[3]	1,323,000	759,000	564,000
1922.......	31,768,000[3]	2,252,000	1,115,000	1,137,000
1923.......	31,290,000[3]	2,162,000	1,355,000	807,000
1924.......	31,056,000[3]	2,068,000	1,581,000	487,000
1925.......	31,064,000[3]	2,038,000	1,336,000	702,000
1926.......	30,784,000[3]	2,334,000	1,427,000	907,000
1927.......	30,281,000[3]	2,162,000	1,705,000	457,000
1928.......	30,275,000[3]	2,120,000	1,698,000	422,000
1929.......	30,257,000[3]	2,081,000	1,604,000	477,000
1930.......	30,169,000[3]	1,723,000	1,740,000	17,000[4]
1931.......	30,585,000[3]	1,469,000	1,683,000	214,000[4]
1932.......	31,241,000[3]	1,011,000	1,544,000	533,000[4]
1933.......	32,242,000[3]	.....	.....	.....

[1] Estimated, United States Census.
[2] Enumerated, United States Census.
[3] Revised estimates, Bureau of Agricultural Economics.
[4] Net movement from cities to farms, a reversal of earlier trend.
NOTE: Births and deaths not taken into account in estimates of the movement.

the country to the city. And since most of the migrants in the other direction--from the city to the country--actually consist of people who at one time had lived on farms, it is evident that what we have had for many years are intolerable conditions in the country driving people out of the country, and then intolerable conditions in the city, driving them back again.

The question to which I have been seeking an answer is whether the way of life described in this book is a way out for a population evidently unhappy both in the city and in the country. Those who are interested in this question, and those who are considering such a way of living, may find in this volume an answer to many of the problems which perplex them in connection with it. Those who are interested in the broader implications of the Borsodi family's quest of comfort in a civilization evidently intolerably uncomfortable will find them fully discussed in *This Ugly Civilization.*

We are living in one of the most interesting periods in the world's history. Industrial civilization is either on the verge of collapse or of rebirth on a new social basis. Men and women who desire to escape from dependence upon the present industrial system and who have no desire to substitute for it dependence upon a state controlled system, are beginning to experiment with a way of living which is neither city life nor farm life, but which is an effort to combine the advantages and to escape the disadvantages of both. Reports of the Department of Agriculture call attention to the revival of handicraft industries—the making of rugs and other textiles, furniture, baskets and pottery--for sale along the roads, in near-by farmers' markets, or for barter for other products for the farm and home. Farmers, according to the Bureau of Home Economics, are turning back to custom milling of flour because they can thus get a barrel of flour for five bushels of wheat, whereas by depending upon the milling industry they have to "pay" eighteen bushels of wheat for the same quantity of flour.

According to the same authority, meat clubs have been growing in number; a heavier canning and preserving program is being carried out; bread-baking, churning, cheese-making and other home food-production activities have been revived; home sewing has increased greatly, and on some farms where sheep are raised, skills and equipment little used for many years are being called upon to convert home-grown wool into clothing and bed coverings; soap-making for family use has increased; farm-produced fuel is being used more freely; lumber made from the farm wood-lot is being used for repairs to the house and for furniture-making. The movement toward subsistence farming is receiving extraordinary official recognition and support. President Roosevelt flatly and frankly announces as a major policy of his administration and as a primary purpose of his life to *put into effect a back-to-the-land movement that will work.* "There is a necessary limit," he said early in 1930, "to the continuance of the migration from the country to the city, and I look, in fact, for a swing of the pendulum in the other direction. All things point that way.... The great objective ... aims at making country life in every way as desirable as city life--an objective which will, from the economic side, make possible the earning of an adequate compensation, and on the social side, the enjoyment of all the necessary advantages which exist today in the cities." Under the President's leadership, appropriations by the Congress for the promotion of subsistence farming and for the development of self-help organizations have already been made.

In Dayton, Ohio, for nearly a year, a sociological experiment of far-reaching significance has been under way. In this industrial city, the support of the Council of Social Agencies has been given to an organized movement based upon production for use (as contrasted with production for the market), and for homesteading with domestic production, as described in this book. As consulting economist for the Dayton movement, it has been my privilege to watch a development which promises, because of the interest other cities are taking in it, to make social history. The recent development of the homestead movement in Dayton is described in the chapter entitled "Postlude," a sort of postscript to this book. Even if this movement fails to develop a new and better social order, as many of those working in it have faith that it will, there is no doubt in my mind that innumerable families will be helped by it to a more secure, more independent, more expressive way of life.

RALPH BORSODI

Chapter One - Flight from the City

IN 1920 the Borsodi family--my wife, my two small sons, and myself--lived in a *rented* home. We *bought* our food and clothing and furnishings from retail stores. We were *dependent* entirely upon my income from a none too certain white-collar job.

We lived in New York City--the metropolis of the country. We had the opportunity to enjoy the incredible variety of foodstuffs which pour into that great city from every corner of the continent; to live in the most luxurious apartments built to house men and women in this country; to use the speedy subways, the smart restaurants, the great office buildings, the libraries, theaters, public schools--all the thousand and one conveniences which make New York one of the most fantastic creations in the history of man. Yet in the truest sense, we could not enjoy any of them.

How could we enjoy them when we were financially insecure and never knew when we might be without a job; when we lacked the zest of living which comes from real health and suffered all the minor and sometimes major ailments which come from too much excitement, too much artificial food, too much sedentary work, and too much of the smoke and noise and dust of the city; when we had to work just as hard to get to the places in which we tried to entertain ourselves as we had to get to the places in which we worked; when our lives were barren of real beauty--the beauty which comes only from contact with nature and from the growth of the soil, from flowers and fruits, from gardens and trees, from birds and animals?

We couldn't. Even though we were able for years and years, like so many others, to forget the fact--to ignore it amid the host of distractions which make up city life.

And then in 1920, the year of the great housing shortage, the house in which we were living was sold over our heads. New York in 1920 was no place for a houseless family. Rents, owing to the shortage of building which dated back to the World War, were outrageously high. Evictions were epidemic--to enable rapacious landlords to secure higher rents from new tenants—and most of the renters in the city seemed to be in the courts trying to secure the protection of the Emergency Rent Laws. We had the choice of looking for an equally endurable home in the city, of reading endless numbers of classified advertisements, of visiting countless real estate agents, of walking weary miles and climbing endless flights of steps, in an effort to rent another home, or of flight from the city. And while we were trying to prepare ourselves for the struggle with this typical city problem, we were overcome with longing for the country--for the security, the health, the leisure, the beauty we felt it must be possible to achieve there. Thus we came to make the experiment in living which we had often discussed but which we had postponed time and again because it involved so radical a change in our manner of life.

Instead, therefore, of starting the irritating task of house and apartment hunting, we wrote to real estate dealers within commuting distance of the city. We asked them for a house which could be readily remodeled; a location near the railroad station because we had no automobile; five to ten acres of land with fruit trees, garden space, pasturage, a woodlot, and if possible a brook; a location where electricity was available, and last but not least, a low purchase price. Even if the place we could afford only barely complied with these specifications, we felt confident that we could achieve economic freedom on it and a degree of comfort we never enjoyed in the city. All the other essentials of the good life, not even excepting

Where the experiment started. The house and barns on "Sevenacres," taken after they were remodelled. the chicken-house back of the barn was the first carpentry work undertaken. After that, shifting the door on the house from the end and replacing it with a window, building the pergola on one end, and putting up the window boxes and side-lights became easy.

schooling for our two sons, we decided we could produce for ourselves if we were unable to buy in a neighborhood which already possessed them.

We finally bought a place located about an hour and three-quarters from the city. It included a small frame house, one and a half stories high, containing not a single modern improvement--there was no plumbing, no running water, no gas, no electricity, no steam heat. There were an old barn, and a chicken-house which was on the verge of collapse, and a little over seven acres of land. There was a little fruit in the orchard--some apples, cherries, and plums, but of the apples at least there were plenty. An idea of the modesty of the first Borsodi homestead can be secured from the picture on page 64, though the picture shows it after we had spent nearly two years repainting and remodeling the tiny little building. Yet "Sevenacres," as we called the place, was large enough for our initial experiment. Four years later we were able to select a more suitable site and begin the building of the sort of home we really wanted.

We began the experiment with three principal assets, courage-- foolhardiness, our city friends called it; a vision of what modern methods and modern domestic machinery might be made to do in the way of eliminating drudgery, and the fact that my wife had been born and had lived upto her twelfth year on a ranch in the West. She at least had had childhood experience of life in the country.

But we had plenty of liabilities. We had little capital and only a modest salary. We knew nothing about raising vegetables, fruit, and poultry. All these things we had to learn. While I was a handy man, I had hardly ever had occasion to use a hammer and saw (a man working in an office rarely does), and yet if our experiment was to succeed it required that I should make myself a master of all trades. We cut ourselves off from the city comforts to which we had become so accustomed, without the countryman's material and spiritual compensations for them.

We went to the country with nothing but our city furniture. We began by adding to this wholly unsuitable equipment for pioneering, an electric range. This was the first purchase in the long list of domestic machines with which we proposed to test our theory that it was possible to be more comfortable in the country than in the city, with security, independence, and freedom to do the work to which we aspired thrown in for good measure.

Discomforts were plentiful in the beginning. The hardships of those early years are now fading into a romantic haze, but they were real enough at the time. A family starting with our handicaps had to expect them. But almost from the beginning there were compensations for the discomforts.

Before the end of the first year, the year of the depression of 1921 when millions were tramping the streets of our cities looking for work, we began to enjoy the feeling of plenty which the city-dweller never experiences. We cut our hay; gathered our fruit; made gallons and gallons of cider. We had a cow, and produced our own milk and butter, but finally gave her up. By furnishing us twenty quarts of milk a day she threatened to put us in the dairy business. So we changed to a pair of blooded Swiss goats. We equipped a poultry-yard, and had eggs, chickens, and fat roast capons. We ended the year with plenty not only for our own needs but for a generous hospitality to our friends--some of whom were out of work--a hospitality which, unlike city hospitality, did not involve purchasing everything we served our guests.

To these things which we produced in our first year, we have since added ducks, guineas, and turkeys; bees for honey; pigeons for appearance; and dogs for company. We have in the past twelve years built three houses and a barn from stones picked up on our place; we weave suitings, blankets, carpets, and draperies; we make some of our own clothing; we do all of our own laundry work; we grind flour, corn meal, and breakfast cereals; we have our own workshops, including a printing plant; and we have a swimming-pool, tennis-court, and even a billiard-room.

In certain important respects our experiment was very different from the ordinary back-to-the-land adventure. We quickly abandoned all efforts to raise anything to sell. After the first year, during which we raised some poultry for the market, this became an inviolable principle. We produced only for our own consumption. If we found it difficult to consume or give away any surplus, we cut down our production of that particular thing and devoted the time to producing something else which we were then buying. We used machinery wherever we could, and tried to apply the most approved scientific methods to small-scale production. We acted on the theory that there was always some way of doing what we wanted to do, if we only sought long enough for the necessary information, and that efficient machinery would pay for itself in the home precisely as it pays for itself in the factory.

The part which domestic machinery has played in making our adventure in homesteading a success cannot be too strongly emphasized. Machinery enabled us to eliminate drudgery; it furnished us skills which we did not possess, and it reduced the costs of production both in terms of money and in terms of labor. Not only do we use machines to pump our water, to do our laundry, to run our refrigerator--we use them to produce food, to produce clothing, to produce shelter.

Some of the machines we have purchased have proved unsatisfactory--something which is to be expected since so little real thought has been devoted by our factory-dominated inventors and engineers to the development of household equipment and domestic machinery. But taking the machines and appliances which we have used as a whole, it is no exaggeration to say that we started our quest of comfort with all the discomforts possible in the country, and, because of the machines, we have now achieved more comforts than the average prosperous city man enjoys.

What we have managed to accomplish is the outcome of nothing but a conscious determination to use machinery for the purpose of eliminating drudgery from the home and to produce for ourselves enough of the essentials of living to free us from the thralldom of our factory-dominated civilization.

What are the social, economic, political, and philosophical implications of such a type of living? What would be the consequence of a widespread transference of production from factories to the home?

If enough families were to make their homes economically productive, cash-crop farmers specializing in one crop would have to abandon farming as a business and go back to it as a way of life. The packinghouses, mills, and canneries, not to mention the railroads, wholesalers, and retailers, which now distribute agricultural products would find their business confined to the production and distribution of exotic foodstuffs. Food is our most important industry. A war of attrition, such as we have been carrying on all alone, if extended on a large enough scale, would put the food industry out of its misery, for miserable it certainly is, all the way from the farmers who produce the raw materials to the men, women, and children who toil in the canneries, mills, and packing-towns, and in addition reduce proportionately the congestion, adulteration, unemployment, and unpleasant odors to all of which the food industry contributes liberally.

If enough families were to make their homes economically productive, the textile and clothing industries, with their low wages, seasonal unemployment, cheap and shoddy products, would shrink to the production of those fabrics and those garments which it is impractical for the average family to produce for itself.

If enough families were to make their homes economically productive, undesirable and non-essential factories of all sorts would disappear and only those which would be desirable and essential because they would be making tools and machines, electric light bulbs, iron and copper pipe, wire of all kinds, and the myriad of things which can best be made in factories, would remain to furnish employment to those benighted human beings who prefer to work in factories.

Domestic production, if enough people turned to it, would not only annihilate the undesirable and nonessential factory by depriving it of a market for its products. It would do more. It would release men and women from their present thralldom to the factory and make them masters of machines instead of servants to them; it would end the power of exploiting them which ruthless, acquisitive, and predatory men now possess; it would free them for the conquest of comfort, beauty and understanding.

Chapter Two - Domestic Production

WITH Newton, it was the falling of an apple which led to the discovery of gravitation. With Watts, it was the popping of the lid of a boiling kettle which led to the invention of the steam-engine. With the Borsodi family, it was the canning of tomatoes which led to the discovery of domestic production. Out of that discovery came not only an entirely new theory of living; it led to my writing several books dealing with various phases of the discovery—*National Advertising vs. Prosperity* was the first; then came *The Distribution Age,* finally *This Ugly Civilization.*

In the summer of 1920--the first summer after our flight from the city--Mrs. Borsodi began to can and preserve a supply of fruits and vegetables for winter use. I remember distinctly the pride with which she showed me, on my return from the city one evening, the first jars of tomatoes which she had canned. But with my incurable bent for economics, the question "Does it really pay?" instantly popped into my head. Mrs. Borsodi had rather unusual equipment for doing the work efficiently. She cooked on an electric range; she used a steam-pressure cooker; she had most of the latest gadgets for reducing the labor to a minimum.

I looked around the kitchen, and then at the table covered with shining glass jars filled with tomatoes and tomato juice.

"It's great," I said, "but does it really pay?"

"Of course it does," was her reply.

"Then it ought to be possible to prove that it does--even if we take into consideration every cost--the cost of raw materials, the value of the labor put into the work yourself, the fuel, the equipment."

"That ought to be easy," she maintained.

It didn't prove as easy as we anticipated. We spent not only that evening, but many evenings, trying to arrive at a fairly accurate answer to the question. It wasn't even easy to arrive at a satisfactory figure on the cost of raw materials she had used. Some of the tomatoes had been grown in our own garden; some had been purchased. How much had it cost us to produce the tomatoes we had raised? We had kept no figures on gardening costs. Even if we had kept track of all the odd times during which we had worked in the garden, that would have helped little without a record of the time put into caring for the single row of tomato plants we had planted.

It proved equally difficult to determine how much time should be charged to the actual work of canning--since several different kinds-of household tasks in addition to canning were often performed at the same time. While the jars were processing in the pressure cooker, work having nothing to do with canning was often performed.

And when it came to determining how much electric current had been used--how much to charge for salt, spices, and other supplies--the very smallness of the quantities used made it difficult to arrive at a figure which approximated the facts. However, by abandoning the effort to determine gardening costs, and labor costs, and substituting the market value for both raw materials and for labor, we did finally come to figures which I felt we might use.

Then we still had the problem of determining what it had cost to buy canned tomatoes; we had to buy canned goods in a number of different stores so as to get a fair average price on the cannery-made product; of making certain that they were of a quality similar to those which we had produced at home, and of reducing the quantity in each can and each jar to some unit which would make comparison possible quantitatively as well as qualitatively. *When we finally made the comparison, the cost of the homemade product was between 20 percent and 30 per cent lower than the price of the factory-made merchandise.*

The result astonished me. That there would be a saving, if no charge were made for labor, I expected. I was prepared to find that it paid to can tomatoes whenever the cash income of a family was so low that anything which might be secured for the housewife's labor was a gain. But after every item of expense had been taken into account, and after analyzing the costs of domestic production as carefully as I would have analyzed similar costs in such a cannery as that of the Campbell Soup Company, that a saving should be shown was astonishing. How was it possible, I kept asking myself, for a woman, working all alone, to produce canned goods at a lower cost than could the Campbell Soup Company with its fine division of labor, its efficient management, its labor-saving machinery, its quantity buying, its mass-production economies? Unless there was some mistake in our calculations this experiment knocked all the elaborate theories framed by economists to explain the industrial revolution, into a cocked hat. Unless we had failed to take some element of which I was ignorant into consideration, the economic activities of mankind for nearly two hundred years had been based upon a theory as false as its maritime activities prior to the discovery of the fact that the world was round.

Slowly I evolved an explanation of the paradox. First I sought for it in advertising. I wrote a whole book, *National Advertising vs. Prosperity,* about my excursions into the much-neglected field of advertising economics. Advertising, however, furnished only a partial answer to the question. While I did come to the conclusion that certain kinds of advertising involved economic wastes, I discovered that the bulk of advertising had no more effect upon prices than any other activities incidental to the creation of time and place utilities. Articles discussing my analysis of the economics of advertising were published in the trade press in 1922; my book appeared a year later, in 1923.

My voyage of discovery into the realm of advertising economics led to a deeper search for the truth. Three years later, in 1926, I published the results of several years of study in a book (for which Lew Hahn wrote the introduction), which I called *The Distribution Age.*

Here I came much nearer to a satisfactory explanation of the curious results of our cost studies of home canning. Factory production costs had, it is true, decreased year after year as industry had developed. Nothing had developed to stop the factory in its successful competition with handicraft industry, so far as costs of production were concerned. Our economists, therefore, took it for granted that the superiority of the factory in competition with the home would continue indefinitely into the future. What they overlooked, however, was that while production costs decrease year after year, distribution costs increase. The tendency of distribution and transportation to absorb more and more of the economies made possible by factory production was ignored. Transportation, warehousing, advertising, salesmanship, wholesaling, retailing--all these aspects of distribution cost more than the whole cost of fabricating the goods themselves. Less than one-third of what the consumer pays when actually buying goods at retail is paid for the raw materials and costs of manufacturing finished commodities; over two-thirds is paid for distribution. While we were busily reducing the amount of labor needed to produce things--as the technocrats recently discovered--we were busily engaged in increasing the numbers employed to transport, and sell, and deliver the products which we were consuming. That a time might come when all the economies of factory production would be lost in the cost of getting the product from the points of production to the points of consumption had been generally ignored.

Eventually I stumbled on an economic law which still seems to me the only satisfactory explanation of our adventure with the canned tomatoes: *Distribution costs tend to move in inverse relationship to production costs.* The more production costs are reduced in our factories, the higher distribution costs on factory products become. At some point in the case of most products a time comes when it is cheaper to produce them individually than to buy them factory made. Nothing that we can do to lower distribution costs by increasing the efficiency of our railroads, and nothing that we can do to eliminate competition as socialists propose, upsets this law. As long as we stick to the industrial production of goods this law is operative.

A simple illustration makes this clear. With factory production, large quantities of one product are made in one spot. To use automatic machinery, to divide labor most efficiently, to transport raw materials inexpensively, it is necessary to manufacture in quantity. Raw materials and fuel most therefore be assembled from long distances before the process of fabrication can begin. After the raw materials have been fabricated into finished goods--a process which may require movement of the semi-manufactured goods back and forth among several plants located at different points of the country--the finished goods must be transported and stored at the points of consumption until the public is ready to use them. The larger factories are made in order to lower production costs, the greater become the distances and the more intricate the problems involved in assembling the raw materials and distributing the finished goods. Thus the lower we make the factory costs, the higher become the distribution costs.

It cost the Campbell Soup Company much less to produce a can of tomatoes in their great factories than it cost Mrs. Borsodito produce one in her kitchen. But after they had produced theirs, all the costs of getting it from their factory to the ultimate consumer had to be added. In Mrs. Borsodi's case the first cost was the final cost. No distribution costs had to be added because the point of production and the point of consumption was the same.

All the orthodox economic teachings to which I had subscribed underwent a complete transformation as soon as I fully digested the implications of this discovery.

I discovered that more than two-thirds of the things which the average family now buys could be produced more economically at home than they could be bought factory made; --that the average man and woman could earn more by producing at home than by working for money in an office or factory and that, therefore, the less time they spent working away from home and the more time they spent working at home, the better off they would be; --finally, that the home itself was still capable of being made into a productive and creative institution and that an investment in a homestead equipped with efficient domestic machinery would yield larger returns per dollar of investment than investments in insurance, in mortgages, in stocks and bonds.

The most modern and expensive domestic machinery need not, therefore, be a luxury. It can be a productive investment, in spite of the fact that most manufacturers of appliances still sell their machines on the basis of a luxury appeal. Even appliances like vacuum cleaners can be made paying investments, if the time they save is used productively in the garden, the kitchen, the sewing and loom room.

These discoveries led to our experimenting year after year with domestic appliances and machines. We began to experiment with the problem of bringing back into the home, and thus under our own direct control, the various machines which the textile-mill, the cannery and packing house, the flour-mill, the clothing and garment factory, had taken over from the home during the past two hundred years. Needless to say, we have thus far only begun to explore the possibilities of domestic production.

In the main the economies of factory production, which are so obvious and which have led economists so far astray, consist of three things: (1) quantity buying of materials and supplies; (2) the division of labor with each worker in industry confined to the performance of a single operation; and (3) the use of power to eliminate labor and permit the operation of automatic machinery. Of these, the use of power is unquestionably the most important. Today, however, power is something which the home can use to reduce costs of production just as well as can the factory. The situation which prevailed in the days when water power and steam-engines furnished the only forms of power is at an end. As long as the only available form of power was *centralized* power, the transfer of machinery and production from the home and the individual, to the factory and the group, was inevitable. But with the development of the gas-engine and the electric motor, power became available in *decentralized* forms. The home, so far as power was concerned, had been put in position to compete with the factory.

With this advantage of the factory nullified, its other advantages are in themselves insufficient to offset the burden of distribution costs on most products. Furthermore, even these advantages are not as great as they seem. What is saved through minute division and subdivision of labor tends often to be nullified by the higher costs of supervision and management. And the savings in the factory made possible by quantity buying become more and more minute when the home begins to produce raw materials itself.

The average factory, no doubt, does produce food and clothing cheaper than we produce them even with our power-driven machinery on the Borsodi homestead. But factory costs, because of the problem of distribution, are only first costs. They cannot, therefore, be compared with home costs, which are final costs. The final cost of factory products, after distribution costs have been added, make the great bulk of consumer goods actually more expensive than home-made products of the same quality.

This is what we learned from Mrs. Borsodi's adventure with the tomatoes.

Chapter Three - Food, Pure Food, And Fresh Food

IT IS a mistake, however, to think of our experiments in domestic production purely in terms of economics. Particularly is this true of food. For ours was not only a revolt against the high cost of food. It was a revolt against the kind of food with which mass production and mass distribution provides the American consumer.

In common with the overwhelming majority of people, we suffered the usual run of digestive and catarrhal ailments. We all had colds several times each year; constipation was something every member of the family had to fight; between periods of biliousness, headaches, fevers, and similar visitations, we enjoyed only what might at best be described as tolerable health. I would not give the impression that we were a sickly family. On the contrary, so far as health was concerned we were probably better rather than worse than the average family. Our ailments were almost never severe enough to keep us in bed. None of us had ever been confined in a hospital. But saying that our health was slightly better than average is not saying much.

Partly as a result of an accumulation of accidents and coincidents, and partly because of our own efforts to find the answer to the riddle of good health, we finally arrived at the conviction that most of our ailments, and probably most of the ailments of mankind, were caused by wrong foods and incorrect eating habits. I remember how amusing this idea sounded the first time it was propounded to me. Mrs. Borsodi and I, happening to meet Hereward Carrington, just as we were on our way to lunch in the city, asked him to join us.

"I'm sorry," he said, "but I seem to be catching cold, so I am eating nothing at all today."

I looked at him with astonishment. The old adage about feeding a cold and starving a fever came into my mind. What in the world, I thought, could eating have to do with a cold? "Join us, anyway," I said. "You can watch us eat, and the sight of food may tempt you to order something yourself. And besides, I'm curious to know upon what theory you cut out eating when you have a cold."

Carrington accepted the invitation and in the course of that luncheon Mrs. Borsodi and I listened for the first time to a disinterested exponent of the theory that improper eating is the cause of most disease. Up to that time I had always dismissed the idea as the vaporing of vegetarian and physical culture faddists. But I was by no means convinced by what Carrington said. I still argued valiantly for the orthodox medical explanation of disease in terms of germs. The luncheon failed to convert us to the extreme position which he maintained and which we have since come to accept. But the incident prepared us for real conversion shortly thereafter.

Among the books published by the corporation by which I was then employed were a number of volumes by a Dr. R. L. Alsaker. I had never read them, principally because they had seemed to me the works of a dietetic crank. But I brought some of them home after the Carrington argument and Mrs. Borsodi and I both read them. Alsaker's arguments seemed to us quite reasonable. We saw no reason why we should hesitate about experimenting with diet as a means of maintaining health, the medical profession having signally failed to keep us healthy. But we did not find this as easy as might be imagined. Indeed, it was only after a period of years and after we had moved to the country that we completely changed our diet from the conventional pattern to our present one. During this period Mrs. Borsodi made quite a study of the chemistry of food; we dug up what we could about the fight for pure and unadulterated foods which Dr. Harvey W. Wiley had waged back in President Theodore Roosevelt's administration, and as a result developed a thoroughgoing distaste for the commercialized foodstuffs which up to that time we had eaten.

One after another we gave up predigested breakfast foods, white bread, factory-made biscuits and crackers and cakes, polished rice, white sugar. But it wasn't easy to secure suitable substitutes for all the foods which we believed unfit for human consumption. What should we do in order to secure clean, raw milk, fresh vegetables, and decent chickens? The pasteurized milk which we had been drinking for years was a crime against the human stomach even though the germs which got into the milk in the course of its progress from the cow-stable to our back doors were all embalmed and thus rendered harmless. The fresh vegetables and fruits in the city markets were of necessity of inferior qualities; they had to be picked green, before they ripened naturally, in order to make it possible to transport them without too much spoilage. In addition, they withered and dried out while being shipped, stored and displayed for sale. Meat came to us from a spick and span butcher shop, but we could never forget that it had first passed through the packing-houses which Upton Sinclair had called "the jungle." After we moved to the country and acquired the habit of eating fresh-killed chicken, we could hardly force ourselves to eat chicken in the city. Nothing which a cook can do to a chicken in the kitchen can disguise for us the flavor which develops in a chicken after it has been kept for weeks and possibly for many months in cold storage with all its intestines intact inside. In the course of our studies of diet we became conscious for the first time of the fact that all these things were part and parcel of city living and of the factory packing of foodstuffs to which industrialism seemed to have irretrievably condemned the consuming public.

Actually our moving to the country was inspired less by the notion that we could reduce the cost of living than by the conviction that we could live better than we had in the city. So far as food was concerned, better health was more in our minds than saving money. We sought pure food and fresh food rather than cheap food. The discovery that home production made it possible for us to enjoy better food at a lower cost than we had in the city, came later.

We landed in the country on April 1st, a little late in the season, we have since learned for starting chickens. But since raising chickens was almost the first item in our food raising program, we went ahead, anyway. Eggs had always been an important factor in our dietary, we wanted to have plenty of them, and the supply of fresh chicken which would accompany egg production would, we felt, cut down what we had been in the habit of spending for meat of all kinds.

We knew nothing about chickens. For instructions we turned to the bulletins of the Department of Agriculture in Washington and of the state agricultural university. We pored over bulletins dealing with incubation, with raising chicks, with feeding hens for egg production and fattening poultry for the table. We followed in a general way the instructions in the bulletins about equipment and housing them. But we nevertheless decided to feel our way and to try out our book-taught knowledge before venturing on any considerable investment in our poultry-yard. Unless experienced personal guidance is available, no amount of mere reading can prevent the beginner from making mistakes. If the initial venture is a large one, the mistake may prove financially disastrous. Some years after we moved to the country, a small, completely equipped farm near us was purchased by another city migrant. Ill-health and inability to keep up his work in the city (he was a newspaper man)had forced this move upon him. It was his idea to raise chickens for a living. He, too, started out knowing nothing about chickens and having to rely upon book knowledge for information. But unlike the Borsodi family, he started out on a large scale, buying 100-day-old chicks from commercial hatcheries to begin. The poultry books told him that the chicks were to be fed grit and water before they received their first regular feed. To a countryman, the word grit would have been self-explanatory. No doubt the author of the bulletin upon which this man relied did not feel it necessary to explain what grit was, or, if there was such an explanation in the book, its significance did not register on our neighbor. At any rate, what he did do was to go to his barns and look for a sack of grit. Having found what he thought was grit, he proceeded to feed it to his chickens as instructed. Within a short time the chickens began to die right and left. He began to lose chicks in batches of fifty in a single day. And he had hardly any of his original loo chicks left when he discovered that what he had thought grit, in reality was linseed meal. Here was the first of what proved a series of catastrophic losses for this family. Precious money and even more precious time was lost, owing to this mistake. Before this man learned enough about living in the country to produce with any degree of efficiency (though I believe nothing could have enabled him to produce profitably for the market), his losses were so great that he had to abandon the place he had purchased and to return to the city, broken in pocket and even more broken in spirit. I cannot, therefore, make this point too strongly--the only alternative to experienced guidance is experimenting on a small scale. Mistakes then can be considered part of one's education.

It is difficult today, when the care of our poultry-yard takes so little original thinking on our part, to realize how bewildered we were when we first began with chickens. There was, to begin with, the problem of breeds. Roughly, all the various breeds of chickens fall into three categories: egg-laying machines, like the Leghorns; meat-making chickens, like the Jersey Giants; and all-purpose breeds, like the Plymouth Rocks and the Rhode Island Reds. The Leghorns do lay more eggs than the other types, but they are small and wiry birds, hardly fit for the table. As we wanted plenty of eggs, we decided against the Jersey Giants. To secure both eggs and decent meat, we finally decided on one of the all-purpose breeds, Rhode Island Reds, a decision we have never regretted. The Reds are probably no better than others of the same general type; there was no special reason for selecting them unless it was that it was easier for us to get hens and eggs of this breed in our neighborhood than the others.

We started operations that first spring with a broody hen and a setting of eggs which we purchased from a neighbor. Later, we repeated this purchase three or four times. But the first hen had not finished hatching out her setting (it takes three weeks) when we decided that hatching eggs out nature's way wouldn't give us enough chicks for our needs. We purchased a sixty-egg incubator, heated by a kerosene-lamp. While we still set hens, perhaps because "breaking up" broody hens each year is almost as much trouble as setting them, we believe a good, small incubator an essential part of an ideal homestead. We purchased eggs enough to fill the incubator twice that year from farmers who had flocks of Reds. And we managed to hatch out an exceptionally large proportion of them. My recollection is that we started our poultry-yard that first year with about 150 chicks.

This number dwindled down, as is to be expected, to about 100 chickens--half of them pullets and half of them cockerels. The first year we killed a good many of the cockerels for fries in the course of the summer. But the second year we came to the conclusion that this was a most wasteful proceeding, and ordered a set of instruments for caponizing. Eventually every member of the family learned how to caponize the cockerels. The operation is rather interesting; it need never be bloody; and by fattening the capons for six or eight months, we had eight- and nine-pound capons to eat--a luxury which we had never enjoyed at home in the city. Indeed, when I came across Philadelphia capons on restaurant menus, I hadn't the least notion what a capon really was; vaguely I thought them some particularly choice breed of chicken.

The annual food contribution of our poultry-yard, after it was once established, usually averages twenty or twenty-five capons, an equal number of old hens, and all the eggs we can eat. There is always a surplus of eggs in the spring. Sometimes we sell them or turn them in to our grocer, but usually we prefer to put them down and preserve them in water glass, which keeps them fit for cooking purposes for the fall and winter when the production of fresh eggs falls short of our needs. However, if the chicken-house is of warm construction and especially if it is electrically lighted in the winter so as to give the hens a full day at the feed-boxes, a plentiful supply of fresh eggs can be secured the year round.

A small flock of chickens, kept up each year by raising about seventy-five chicks, is all that the average family needs. The dividends per dollar of investment are really enormous, even if all the feed for them has to be purchased. Owing to the fact that land in our section is not adapted to grain farming and the fact that we have had to clear every bit of land for garden purposes, we have purchased nearly all of our chicken feed. There is no reason, however, why the feed should not be produced on the homestead if the soil is suitable. This simply increases the dividends earned and proportionately reduces the family's dependence upon income and purchases from the outside. The labor of feeding and caring for such a flock of chickens is not great, especially if good equipment and housing is provided. A large poultry project, from which money is to be made, is an altogether different affair. The poultry business seems to have a universal popularity. It looks like an easy way to make a living. But it takes much more experience and much more ability than the average man possesses to make money at it. We tried it one year and, while we lost no money on the project (on the contrary, by ordinary standards it might have been considered a success), it was one of the experiences which made us decide against the home production of anything for sale.

A few years after we moved to the country a brother of mine was ordered to the country by his doctor. We invited him to come to "Sevenacres" and suggested that he make his expenses by raising eggs and chickens for the market. So that year we had the opportunity of watching what happened when the flock grew in size to something like commercial proportions. The eggs raised sold well and at high prices. The cockerels were all caponized and in the fall sold to a restaurant in the city. Yet when we were all through with the year there was precious little to show for the labor which had been put into them.

By the time that feed and supplies were paid for, pocket money was all that my brother had to show for his summer's work. The experiment was well worth while, however, because it proved one of the things which helped us to decide that any extra time which we could put into production could be more profitably used raising other things for our own use than by raising a surplus of one thing, such as eggs and chickens, for sale.

We have applied this principle to the poultry-yard itself, keeping the number of chickens down and raising other fowls. We have raised Peking ducks and found that the Peking duck furnishes almost as many eggs as do many breeds of chickens, and in addition furnishes a welcome variation in the diet. We also raise turkeys; we plan to raise at least one bird for each month for the table, and a flock to be used as Christmas presents. This particular experiment in the home production of gifts has been among our most successful; the sentiment surrounding the turkeys savors of Christmas much more than factory-made gadgets usually bought in crowded stores. We have also raised pigeons, principally because they were decorative, and have hatched pheasants principally for the sake of romance. It is part of our yearly spring thrill to watch for the first appearance of the cock pheasants and to see them in all their finery as they begin their courting dances.

A few words must be added on the subject of fresh eggs. We used to buy so-called fresh eggs in the city, but in the very nature of things it was impossible for them to be really fresh. Even near-by eggs rarely get to the city before they are two weeks old. True, the palate of the city man is so little cultivated that the finer flavors of all sorts of foods have lost their importance to him. Industrialism and urbanism have combined to blunt his taste. As to fresh eggs, the Borsodi family consists of gourmets. The fact that the humble egg has developed a new value for us is typical of the transvaluations which have come to us from our return to nature.

Milk, cream, buttermilk, butter, cheese, ice-cream--all the various milk products--constituted one of the large items in our food budget when we lived in the city. Our fluid milk supply consisted of grade A milk, delivered daily in glass bottles. This milk was pasteurized. We used creamery butter which at that time was made from raw cream. Since then efforts have been made to compel creameries to use only pasteurized milk. Buttermilk we drank only occasionally. After we moved to the country it became a part of our regular diet; it proved a most healthful and nourishing foodstuff. Ice-cream we ate in much greater moderation in the city than we do today, perhaps because of some Puritanical inhibition about eating too much dessert. But probably the notion was actually correct, at least with regard to commercial ice-cream, which is what we used to eat. Certainly the bulk of commercial ice-cream, often made from rancid cream, artificial coloring, and synthetic flavoring, is not a desirable food. But even the best commercial ice-cream cannot be compared with home-made ice-cream and frozen desserts made from clean, sweet cream, fresh eggs, and real fruit juices. Much of the cheese now consumed in the city is synthetic, made from something which the breweries invented and which ought not to be called cheese at all. We ate little cheese before we left the city; after we went to the country we began to eat all the pot cheese we could enjoy, and when we learned how useful a part of the diet cheese can be, we began to buy the kinds of cheese which we could not make at home.

Our revolt against commercial milk products was helped by one of those fortuitous incidents which shape all of our lives, though we are seldom conscious of their importance at the time. Mrs. Borsodi, before she gave up business, had occasion to visit one of the largest creameries in the country to secure information for an advertising campaign. Her disillusionment about the dairy industry and creamery butter was complete. Modern science, she found, was being used to produce a tasty and attractive-looking butter from raw materials which often came into the creamery only fit for slopping to hogs. Of superficial cleanliness there was plenty, but underneath the scrupulous surface was the fact that the system was so perfect that no matter what sort of cream was used, a product which had the appearance of quality was produced. No doubt in a perfectly organized industrial state, in which the profit motive has in some way been legislated out of existence, the technicians who will operate the creameries will eliminate some of the worst of present-day mass-production evils. We, however, were not only somewhat cynical about the benefits of unlimited government supervision, but saw no good reason why we should postpone the eating of pure and fresh foods until the distant day when a social revolution would wipe out all the blots on present-day industrial production. Besides, contacts with state institutions-- hospitals, for instance--prevented us from sharing the sanguine hopes of socialist friends about the quality of foodstuffs which would be produced in a socialist heaven.

As soon as we were well settled in the country we bought a cow--too good a cow, I am afraid. When fresh she gave us as much as twenty quarts of milk a day. Most of the time we had so much milk that it seemed as if we could bathe in it. But what milk it was! In spite of the fact that we drank all we desired, made our own butter and pot cheese, there was still a surplus of milk to be disposed of. A few neighbors begged us to sell them milk, but this experience, just like our experience in selling eggs and chickens, only confirmed our determination not to produce for the market. We were producing a quality of milk far superior to that in the market; what we received for it hardly paid for the labor of cleaning bottles and delivering it. We wondered what we could buy with the money half so precious as the milk. We needed two or three quarts of milk daily. Twenty was too much of a good thing. We had no intention of living on milk alone, nor of going into the dairy business. For a family of four, the cow was evidently not the best solution of the milk problem. With a family of six or more persons, it would perhaps have been different. But for us, using a cow to produce milk was like using a sledge hammer to drive carpet tacks. We sold the cow and decided to try Swiss milch goats.

The milch goat is still somewhat of a novelty, handicapped by the fact that the goat is supposed to be funny. In our judgment it is an ideal solution of the problem of producing milk for use within the family. Its milk is richer than cow's milk in butter fat, and easier to digest. When the goats are properly fed, it is hard to distinguish its taste from cow's milk. We have repeatedly fooled friends of ours who were prejudiced against it. We bought one pure-blooded Toggenburg doe, and one grade doe. The grade doe was probably a half-blood; there is no reason why one should go to the expense of buying pure bloods unless one intends to go into goat-breeding. Properly selected grade goats will give practically as much milk and are much less expensive. Two does, however, should be purchased. Goats are evidently very gregarious; they fret and hold back their milk if they are without companionship. The buck is a smelly and obnoxious animal, and the does should be taken to a buck when ready for breeding. Unlike a cow, which is a perfect nuisance when in heat, bellowing and carrying on in a most disgraceful manner, the does are so small that they can be put into any automobile and quickly taken to a buck for breeding. By breeding one doe so that it kids in the spring and the other in the fall, two does will furnish a supply of milk the year round. When fresh, our does gave us about three quarts of milk daily.

Among the great advantages of the goats was the great reduction in the labor of milking and caring for them. To milk a quart or two morning and evening proved a trifling job in comparison with having to fill a ten-quart pail twice a day. And the goats, unlike the cow, kept themselves clean. As a matter of fact, they are rather fastidious in their habits. They will not eat grain or hay which has been trampled under foot, though they will eat almost any kind of vegetation and are fond of eating the bark off of trees. This partiality for bark probably explains their fondness for paper, most of which is made of wood pulp. They will probably eat the paper off of a tin can, but the notion that they will eat the tin itself seems to me a silly superstition.

One disadvantage of goats has to do with butter. The fat globule in goat's milk does not separate or rise as readily as that in cow's milk. If butter is to be made, a cream separator has to be used. With this piece of apparatus to overcome this disadvantage, it seems to me that for the small family all the advantages lie on the side of the goat. We found butter-making, using an efficient rotary churn, a most profitable activity.

There is simply no comparison between fresh, homemade butter and creamery butter. With a good refrigerator to get the cream to the proper temperature, the butter forms very quickly. Most of the operations in butter-making can be done mechanically with an efficient kitchen mixer.

When we purchased "Sevenacres,"we found ourselves in possession of a small "farm" little of which was really suitable for farming. There was plenty of room for garden, though no vegetables and berries had been raised on the place for many years; there was an old orchard containing some apple, plum, and cherry trees; there was a hay-field, and a piece of woodland suitable for a wood-lot. Actual farming operations for us, when we began to develop our theory of self- sufficiency, seemed to fall into two divisions—one having to do with the growing of vegetables, berries, fruit, and foodstuffs for our own consumption, and the other with the growing of feed for the chickens, the goats, and other livestock. We have had considerable success with the first; with the second we have tried to do relatively little as yet.

During the four years we were on "Sevenacres" we did not get around to grain-farming at all, though there was room enough for raising grain enough for both feed and for our own table. On the "Dogwoods" we have not as yet cleared enough ground. We have always managed to produce some hay, and on our new place have usually managed to put away a load of oats each year which we fed to the Toggenborgs. Eventually we hope to produce all our own feed, as we believe it thoroughly practicable and extremely profitable for homesteaders to do so. An acre devoted to corn and wheat, and a half acre devoted to alfalfa, soy-beans, or clover, would take care of the feed for all the livestock needed by the average family, especially if the fields are well fertilized and properly cultivated. Commercial feed has cost us consistently two or three times as much as farmers in the grain-growing sections of the country receive for corn and other grain. Sometimes it has been four times as high. By the time freight, storage, and handling charges are added to the price the farmer has received, the price has no resemblance to that in the primary markets. Even though it costs the homesteader much more to raise feed than it does the farmer who operates a grain "factory" in the West, it would cost him less to do so than to buy feed.

Since we have raised so little of our feed, what we have actually done with our livestock operations has been to substitute a feed bill monthly for the milk and butter bill, and the egg and poultry bill, which we used to receive in the city. The feed bills, however, have not only been much smaller, but have enabled us to enjoy a quality of dairy and poultry products much higher than we were able to secure in the city. Some day we shall clear away enough stumps and roots on our new place so that we can cut out the feed bill as well. When that time comes, it will be hard for the industrial system to starve us out, no matter how badly business goes to pot.

A completely vegetarian family could live entirely out of a kitchen garden and orchard occupying no more than an acre of land. But we never subscribed to the tenets of this dietetic cult, though we are convinced that the average American family consumes much more meat than good health requires. Most of us, so to speak, are digging our graves with our teeth. Over-eating meat is one of the ways in which the public generally practices this form of suicide. For this reason we have tried to increase our consumption of fruits and vegetables and to decrease correspondingly our consumption of meat. This has made the vegetable garden and the orchard acquire a place of much greater economic importance on our homestead than is usual on the average farm, and to correspondingly decrease the importance of the livestock. For instance, we have never gone in for hog-raising, even though we are fond of pork. Between chickens, ducks, and turkeys, and an occasional "bull" calf or "buck" kid which we did not wish to raise and therefore slaughtered, we have had plenty of meat. When particularly hungry for ham and pork, we patronized the local meat market. Families hungrier for meat than the Borsodi family should raise a couple of pigs each year, buying the young pigs and fattening them for the fall and winter. This would also furnish a plentiful supply of lard, a natural food, instead of the chemical fats which people now use. Butter and chicken fat, however, have enabled us to get along without purchasing any fats except olive oil.

The vegetable garden should be large enough to supply the family with fresh vegetables during the growing season and with enough for canning and dehydrating for the winter. In our garden we go in heavily for staples such as peas, beans, radishes, carrots, lettuce, cabbages, turnips, asparagus, rhubarb, potatoes, and sweet corn, but we have always selected the more toothsome varieties of even these old standbys. The varieties developed for commercial purposes are notable usually for size and color rather than flavor. Sweet corn is an instance of this. For many years we have raised nothing but yellow bantam corn, which we believe far superior in quality to the large, white ears which we used to get in the city markets. Incidentally, sweet corn fresh from the garden, before the sugar in the corn has had a chance to turn into starch, is a very different foodstuff from sweetcorn after it has been shipped to the city and more or less dried out in the process. Even a dull palate has no difficulty in noticing the difference.

Such a garden is a much larger undertaking than the usual suburban backyard project. Unless one is content to devote oneself to back-breaking drudgery, the garden cannot be taken care of with a spade for "plowing" and an old-fashioned hoe for "cultivation." We turned to the wheel hoe, one of the simplest of agricultural implements, for help in reducing the labor to manageable proportions. This relatively inexpensive piece of machinery reduced the labor to a point where it demanded no more of my time and strength than should begiven to some form of exercise regularly every day. The investment of $3.50 to $5, in this implement with its set of attachments of plows, weeders, cultivators and rakes, pays for itself over and over again in a single year. Except when plowing and planting, it makes it possible to use our "man" power without abusing it. In the spring and the fall, when planting or harvesting is under way, the whole family goes to the garden and the heavier labor at that time is turned into a sort of family game. It is an amusing fact that the garden has furnished me exercise for which we had to pay money in the city. There, to keep oneself fit, one has to turn to gymnasiums or to golf.

We have experimented with the use of power in farming. But power is really unnecessary on the scale we have operated. We have a Fordson tractor on our place, but it was purchased only because we had to clear the land on which we built our new home. It more than paid for itself in excavating, in road-making, and in hauling timbers and stones at the "Dogwoods." Even the small garden tractor, which represents an investment of around $200 today, is of doubtful utility unless the homestead goes in for field corn, wheat, and other grains. Then, of course, either a horse or small tractor becomes a paying investment, with the horse perhaps the better of the two under present conditions. It takes money to buy gasoline and oil; the fuel for the horse can be produced on the farm. The horse, too, makes it possible to reduce expenditures for fertilizer. No wonder that since the depression there has been a decided increase in the use of horses for farming and a corresponding decline in the use of tractors.

Both on economic and on nutritional grounds we have revolted against the commercial cereals and ordinary white flour. A small grist-mill, to which we attached a motor from a discarded dishwasher, has made it possible for us to grind our own flour, and to crack cereals for breakfast foods. We have even managed to cut down the cost of the mash we feed to our chickens by buying whole grains and grinding them ourselves. That this simple piece of machinery should be in every homestead can certainly be demonstrated on the basis of what it saves on the cost of whole-wheat flour, which is the only kind we use.

We, of course, have had to buy our wheat. The wheat is, therefore, our first cost. If wheat and oats and corn are grown on the homestead, this would no longer be the first cost. First cost would be whatever we had to spend in labor and money to raise the wheat. After paying for the wheat, and adding the value of the labor and the cost of current and similar expenses of operating our mill, our whole-wheat flour costs us about 1½ cents per pound. Whole-wheat flour of the same quality now sells in the grocery store for 6½ cents per pound. The difference between the two is alone sufficient to make the investment in the flourmill pay us handsome dividends. But the saving on white flour is, I believe, much greater, and consists of other savings than those calculable in terms of money.

We use no white flour, except occasionally for pastry. White flour, I believe, along with white sugar and white rice, is one of the most harmful products for which we are indebted to the factory system. All these bleached and whitened foodstuffs are made white by the mills which produce them not only for the sake of their appearance, but in order to preserve them during the long period of time which elapses between the time when they are ground in the mill and the time they are consumed by the public. Dentists will tell you that these white foods soften the teeth; dietitians and doctors that they cause constipation. Personally, I hold them suspect for the great white plague of tuberculosis.

White flour is only one of the three products into which wheat is converted by our mills. The white flour we consume in bread and pastry; the middlings are bleached and sold to us for breakfast food as Cream of Wheat, and the bran is sold to us in neat packages to cure us of the constipation which the white flour causes. Dr. Kellogg, of the Battle Creek Sanitarium, who first hit on the bright idea of marketing bran for this purpose, has made a fortune out of selling this by-product of modern milling to the deluded American public. Yet as long as they insist upon consuming white flour, the bran is an almost essential purchase. All three of these products are present in the whole wheat flour we use, and which costs us about 1½ cents a pound. When we buy wheat after it has been split into three parts by our milling industry, we pay about 2 cents per pound for the white flour; about 13 cents per pound for the middlings in the form of breakfast food, and 20 cents per pound for the bran.

What is true of wheat is also true of corn. The home grist-mill makes it possible for us to grind our own corn meal at a cost of about 1-1/4 cents per pound. But this is whole corn meal and not the pale ghost of the old-fashioned corn meal of our grandmothers. Yet the desiccated starchy substance which is now sold in our stores as corn meal costs 9 cents per pound. This corn meal is made from the dregs of whole corn after the best part, the germ, has been cut out of it to be chemically treated and turned into glucose and corn syrup. These chemical substances in turn have replaced the honey, the maple sugar, the molasses, and the brown sugar which were consumed in their places years ago, and which it is still possible for each individual family to produce for itself. Industrial production of these foodstuffs, instead of representing progress, has resulted in furnishing us inferior food and at a much higher price.

The American housewife tends constantly to buy more prepared or partly prepared food, and to cook and preserve less and less in her kitchen. After we moved to the country, the Borsodi kitchen showed an exact reversal of the general trend. It was not only the room in which we cooked or heated prepared foods for the table--it became the family cannery and packing-house and creamery. And in such a kitchen, we have found that the average woman could earn much more than most of them were earning in the factories, stores and offices for which so many millions of women have abandoned home-making.

One of our first extravagances when we began to reequip and redesign our kitchen for production was the purchase of a steam pressure cooker--price in 1920, $25. We justified this seeming extravagance with the hope that it could be made into a profitable investment. Today pressure cookers of the same size with many improvements over the type we installed can be purchased for $8.50. This piece of domestic machinery enabled the family to

Canning-time in the kitchen at "Dogwoods House." Note the pressure cooker and the electric mixer, which is being used to shred vegetables.

cut the labor of canning to from one-quarter to one-third of that necessary with old-fashioned methods. Its sterilization proved as reliable as any job of processing in the largest canneries of the country. Without the pressure cooker, canning a sufficient supply for winter would have been as great a labor for us as trying to garden with a spade and hoe. With the pressure cooker it became quite practical to put up four-hundred quarts of vegetables and fruits--an ample supply for a family of our size for the whole winter. In addition to the staples usually canned, the pressure cooker enabled us to can veal, chicken, mushrooms, and gelatine. It made it possible for us to go into the winter with jar after jar of delicacies such as chicken breasts, veal gelatine, and genuine mint jelly. These cost us so little, aside from labor, which the pressure cooker and the kitchen mixer reduced to a minimum, that we soon abandoned the task of making detailed comparisons between the cost of the home-made product and the high-priced and inferior canned goods we formerly consumed.

As time went on we kept adding to the kitchen a good many appliances which are usually considered luxuries. I have mentioned that we purchased an electric range for use in the country. There was no gas available on "Sevenacres"; to cook with oil seemed out of question, while the old-fashioned kitchen range, however desirable in the winter, made kitchens an inferno in summer. Our old electric range, which cost us $75 ten years ago, was finally replaced by a $250 range a few years ago--a range equipped with all the modern controls developed during that period of time. But even here we refused to concede that we were going in for luxuries; we were merely bringing our productive kitchen machinery up to date. A test made at the time the new range was installed confirmed us in our belief that the new range, the $200 kitchen mixer with all sorts of attachments, and the electric refrigerator were all dividend-paying investments. Two complete meals consisting of chicken, string beans, diced carrots, prunes, and chocolate cakes were prepared by Mrs. Borsodi and a demonstrator sent up by the General Electric Company, and served to a group of friends. One of the meals was completely factory made from "boughten" products, with nothing added in the kitchen except heat to the product as they came from the packers, canners, and bakers. The total cost of this meal was $3.46. The other was exactly the same as to menu but completely home-made. After figuring the cost of materials at market prices, electric current, investment on machinery and equipment, and making allowance for the difference in the weight of the two meals, the total cost of the home-made meal was $1.59--a saving of $1.87 on a single meal. This proved a saving of $1.40 cents per hour for the time used in cooking the meal—pretty good earnings in comparison with what most women received in industry. Multiply such savings by the more than one thousand meals which are eaten every year by the average family and it is easy to see why we feel that a well-equipped kitchen is no luxury but an absolute essential to the productive home.

It is, however, possible to stress the economic argument unduly. The kitchen is not only a place in which the average woman can earn money. It is even more one of the places in a home in which she can exercise her creative and artistic faculties. Cookery is an art. It is one of those arts much neglected today because we have so generally subscribed to the fallacy that only that is art which has no utility.

But cookery is even more than art. It is science as well. The chemistry of food is a fascinating subject. And if women but knew it, health is more apt to be maintained by what is done by them in the kitchen than by what all the doctors and druggists can do for their families.

Chapter Four - The Loom and the Sewing-Machine

WHEN I first became interested in the possibilities of home weaving, my father told me a story which I have told over and over again because it illustrates most vividly the economic advantages of what I call domestic production.

When he left his home in Hungary to come to this country he was twenty-five years of age. That was not quite fifty years ago. At the time he left Hungary the sheets which were in use in the family's ancestral home were the same sheets which had been included in the hand-spun and hand-woven linens given to his mother as a wedding gift thirty years before. What is more, at the time he left home they were still in perfect condition and apparently good for a lifetime of further service. After thirty years of continuous service those home-spun, home-woven, home-bleached, and home-laundered sheets were still snowy white, heavy linen of a quality it is impossible to duplicate today.

Now let us contrast the sheets which were in my grandmother's home with the sheets in our home today and in that of practically all of the homes of industrialized America. Compared with the luxurious heavy linen in my grandmother's home, we use a relatively cheap, sleazy, factory-spun, factory-woven and factory-finished sheet, which we used to send out to commercial laundries, and which we replaced about every two years. With domestic laundering they last about twice as long. True, the first cost of our factory-made sheets is much less than the cost of the hand-made linens, but the final and complete cost is much greater and at no time do we have the luxury of using the linens which in my grandmother's home were accepted as their everyday due. I do not know what her linen sheets cost in labor and materials fifty years ago. We pay about $1.25 for ours, and on the basis of commercial laundering, have to purchase new ones every two years. Our expenditure for sheets for thirty years, with a family one-quarter the size of grandmother's, would therefore be $18.75 per sheet--much more, I am sure, than was spent for sheets during the same period of time in my grandmother's home. And at the end of thirty years, we would have nothing but a pile of sleazy cotton rags, while in the old home they still had the original sheets probably good for again as much service.

Before the era of factory spinning and factory weaving, which began with the first Arkwright mill in Nottingham, England, in 1768, fabrics and clothing were made in the homes and workshops of each community. Men raised the flax and wool and then did the weaving. Women did the spinning and later sewed and knitted the yarns into garments of all kinds. The music of the spinning-wheel and the rhythm of the loom filled the land. Perhaps one-third of the time of men and women--one-third of their total time at labor--was devoted to producing yarns and fabrics which they consumed.

In the place of loom-rooms in its homes, America now has thousands of mills employing hundreds of thousands of wage-earners. Many of the wage-earners in these textile mills are children in spite of the campaigns against child labor. And the wages paid by these mills are notoriously the lowest which prevail in industry in this country. Instead of healthy and creative work in the homes, we have monotonous and deadly labor in mills.

A trifle over a third of the production of the cotton industry is used for industrial purposes. It is used by manufacturers in fabricating tires, automobile bodies, electric wire, and similar industrial products. Two-thirds of the production of cotton and nearly all of the production of the silk and wool industry goes to the consumer either as piece goods for home sewing, or cut up into wearing apparel by clothing manufacturers. This means that only to 1 per cent of the total number of factories and workers in the entire industry are engaged in producing for the needs of other industries. All of the rest are doing work which used to be done in the home and much of which might still be done there. And our experiments with sewing and weaving tend to show that it can be done at an actual saving of labor or money.

If all the resources of modern science and industry were to be utilized for the purpose of making the spinning-wheel, the reel, and the loom into really efficient domestic machines (as efficient relatively as is the average domestic sewing-machine), the number of textile-mills which could meet the competition of the home producer would be insignificant. And if modern inventive genius were thus applied to these appliances for weaving, there would be no drudgery in domestic weaving; a saving of time and money would be effected; the quality and design of fabrics would be improved, and everybody of high and low degree would be furnished an opportunity to engage in interesting and expressive work. Such improved machinery would occupy no more space than is now wasted in many homes and the loom-room would give to the home a new practical and economic function.

Our loom, in spite of the attachment of a flying shuttle, which has increased its efficiency greatly, remains one of the most primitive pieces of machinery in our home. There is at present no really efficient domestic loom upon the market. Most of the looms made for what is called "band weaving" with emphasis on the silent word "art," are built upon archaic models or devised so as to make weaving as difficult as possible instead of as easy as possible.

The biggest market for these looms is, I believe, in the institutional field. Weaving is one of the favored methods of "occupational therapy" in the ever-increasing number of institutions for nervous and mental disorders which we are erecting all over the country. The strain of repetitive work in our factories and offices, and the absence of creative and productive work in our homes, particularly for women, children, and the is turning us into a race of neurotics. Weaving is being revived, after a fashion, as a therapeutic measure to restore these unfortunates to health. What a ghastly commentary upon what we have called progress. Having taken the looms out of homes during the past century and transferred them to factories, we now find that the absence of the creative work they used to furnish is producing an ever-increasing number of neurotic men and women, and an endless number of "problem" children. So our physicians are putting the loom into their institutions in order to make the victims of this deprivation well again. Then they turn them, after curing them, back into their loomless homes to break down again.

The looms built for occupational therapy and hand-weaving generally are deliberately designed to increase the amount of manual work which those who operate them have to perform for every yard of cloth produced. As a result the actual production of cloth is slow and laborious. Yet there is no reason why this should be so. The right kind of loom would enable the average family to produce suitings, blankets, rugs, draperies, and domestics of all kinds of a quality superior to those generally produced in factories and on sale in stores at a far lower cost after taking time and all materials and supplies into consideration. The artistic and emotional gains from the practice of this craft would therefore be a clear gain.

In the average home, a loom which will weave a width of a yard is sufficient. Ours is able to handle fabrics up to forty-four inches in width. While many things can be made on a simple two-harness loom, we find the four-harness loom a more useful type because of its greater range of design. But every loom should be equipped with an efficient system for warping, and with a flying shuttle, if it is to enable the home-weaver to compete upon an economic basis with the factory. Neither of these are expensive--in fact, the whole investment in equipment in order to weave need not exceed $75 if one can make the flying shuttle arrangement oneself. The shuttle attachment on my loom was home-made and took me only three or four hours to put together. With such a loom, even an average weaver can produce a yard of cloth an hour--and a speedy weaver, willing to exert himself, can produce thirty yards per day. Since it takes only seven yards of twenty-seven-inch cloth to make a three-piece suit for a man, it is possible to weave the cloth for a suit in a single day on a small loom, and in less than a day on a loom able to handle fifty-four-inch cloth.

Some idea of the possibilities of weaving, even without much experience, can be gained from our first experiences with blankets—one was woven by a friend of mine who had never had any experience at all, in a little less than eight hours. A similar one was the first blanket woven by my son--a somewhat better piece of work--in less than six hours. A third was a somewhat more elaborate affair on which three members of the family each did a turn, and so I have no record of the time it took to weave it. The yarn used in these blankets cost about $2.50 for each blanket-- at a time when blankets of similar quality couldn't have been purchased for many times that sum. Even if the loom is only used occasionally, it will earn handsome dividends on the investment at this rate.

Our experiments in the weaving of woolens for men's and women's clothing have demonstrated the practicability not only of cutting out of the budget most of the expenditures for ready-made garments, but even the expenditures for fabrics. The accompanying illustrations of garments made from fabrics woven in the Borsodi homestead suggest not only the great variety of garments for which it is possible to weave the fabrics, but the fact that they are, if anything, more attractive than those which are usually on sale in retail stores ready-made.

The suit shown in the accompanying picture was made from yarn homespun in the Kentucky mountains; the cloth was woven and finished in our home; the suit was made up by a tailor operating a one-man shop near our place. The yarn cost $4.50; the tailoring $30. I had it appraised by various so-called experts at the time, and they valued it all the way from $60 to $90. One friend, who could not qualify as an expert but who has his suits made by Fifth Avenue tailors, said that he had paid $125 for suits no better than this one. Incidentally, the suiting was the first which I ever wove.

This matter of tailoring brings up one of the amusing follies of modern civilization to which we pay no attention but for which we pay, nevertheless, over and over again. The strictly tailored costumes which men now wear have nothing but

Demonstrating the flying shuttle on the loom. There are no really efficient domestic looms on the market. The flying shuttle was added to this loom on the homestead. With this attachment, a yard of cloth is readily woven in an hour. The suit worn by the demonstrator was a hand spun twill, woven on this loom and made-up by a local tailor.

custom to recommend them. They require great skill in sewing; they are therefore impractical for manufacture at home. Yet they are artistic monstrosities. They do nothing to set off the human form. They are not even utilitarian. Most of the hard work of the world is done by men who wear overalls or cotton garments which are not tailored at all. While suits are practical enough for the work which men do in offices, they are much too hot for indoor use--especially in houses which are steam heated. A foolish convention, however, makes us all wear them. If we, however, once again took the designing of our garments into our own hands, it is possible that something much more attractive and useful might develop. We might experiment with blouses, or even with costumes such as the Chinese wear. And apropos of blouses for men, it is an amusing commentary upon the industrialization of Russian life under the Soviets, that the old Russian blouses, which could be made in any household, are now being replaced by the conventional costume of Western civilization—which has to be made in factories.

With women's garments, the field for weaving and for the needlecrafts, even with prevailing styles, is much broader. The garments illustrated show coats, suits, and dresses all made from fabrics woven in our home. I presume I am rather prejudiced in the matter, but it seems to me that the garments Mrs. Borsodi has produced in our home compare favorably with those which most women buy ready to wear today.

The sewing-machine is a most important piece of domestic machinery It is doubtful whether any other piece of machinery pays larger dividends upon the investment made in it. Yet it remains a tool, to be used when needed and laid aside, perhaps for months at a time, when no sewing has to be done. In combination with the loom, the sewing-machine takes on new significance both economically and artistically. What I have here in mind can be made clear by quoting from an article by Mrs. Borsodi in *The Handicrafter,* which describes one of her suits:

The suit was made from a twill suiting. The yarn was a weaving special; the warp tan No. 136, and the weft a lovely green, No. 755. The weave was a simple twill made with four treadles operated 1, 2. 3, 4 and repeat. Four yards of material 27 inches wide were used. The suit was based upon a Vogue pattern, which was modified in many details. Since I had never before tailored homespun, it took many more hours of time to produce the suit than a second one could possibly take. Immediately upon cutting the material by the pattern, I stitched twice around the cut edges on the sewing-machine. This prevented the material from unraveling. I then proceeded much the same as in making any other coat and dress. Finally, after much pressing into shape, I have a suit which has repeatedly been called very good-looking, and which I know gave me more joy in the weaving and making than I ever had in purchasing a similar product from any store. Outside of fur, it is the warmest coat I have ever worn.

It is difficult to compare the cost with a factory product, because I could not afford to purchase this quality and character of material made up. To get this quality of material one would have to go to an expensive house indeed, and to get this particular style of material at the time I finished the suit, it would have been necessary to go to a stylish and even exclusive house be-cause it was just coming in. Taking all these things into consideration, a valu-ation of No would represent a most conservative price.

In judging the hours spent in weaving and sewing, please remember that this was the first time I had done either, and, even on a second garment of this type, the time of weaving and the time spent in sewing could be consid-erably reduced. Also, I could make an even better-looking suit a second time.

In charging fifty cents an hour for my time, I think I have given the benefit of a relatively high rate to the factory, for few factories pay this price for such operations as were performed. To be sure, the factory has its designers who are well paid, but then I paid for my share of such service in the Vogue pattern upon which I relied for assured fit and style. And in addition to the saving on the suit, I had the pleasure of developing a creation of my own.

One-half pound warp at $3.00	$1.50
One pound of weft	3.00
Two yards of lining at $2.50	5.00
Thread	0.20
Pattern	0.65
Total Materials	**$10.35**
Labor weaving, 5 hours at 50¢	2.50
Labor sewing, 12 hours at 50¢	6.00
Total Cost	**$18.85**

It should be borne in mind that the above costs refer to a period when prices were in general fully twice as high as they are today. Both the cost above as well as the price of a garment with which to compare this suit should therefore be understood as establishing relative savings rather than actual savings today. The record, however, can stand examination no matter from what standpoint it is viewed. It would show a nice dividend upon the investment in domestic machinery even after full allowance is made for the time spent in making the suit. It is significant that the two yards of silk lining--purchased factory made-cost almost as much as all the rest of the fabric for both materials and weaving.

What the sewing-machine alone can do is shown from another record from Mrs. Borsodi's cost book.

This covered an afternoon frock, appraised at the time it was made as worth $49.50.

Three and a half yards of silk	$8.75
Pattern and findings	0.90
Sundries	0.15
Cost exclusive of labor	**$9.80**
Earned in thirteen hours (a more skillful worker could have made the frock in less time), assuming a similar frock could have been purchased for $4g.so and that the time spent in shopping for the ready-made garment	
and the superior fit and individual style of the specially made dress is disregarded	$39.70
Value of afternoon frock	**$49.50**

Some of the value in this frock lay, I presume, in its "style," something for which women pay a great deal if they are intent on keeping on with the latest developments in Paris. The sewing-machine makes it possible to secure style without having to patronize the most expensive stores and to pay a premium for this service.

The coat shown was made on the same warp as the man's suit previously referred to, but with a heavier weft. It cost about $3.50 in yarn and about 24 hours for sewing and weaving. The fabric is a distinctive herringbone effect; it is exceedingly warm; it

Some of the Products of the loom-room and sewing room - On the Left--a dress, and a Suit, two blankets, and a wall hanging. All home woven and home sewn. On the right--a home-woven and home-sewn coat with the yarn home spun in the Kentucky mountains. The hat, the handbag, and even the gloves--which were crocheted--were also homemade. The fabric is a rich, deep red; the weave is a novel Herringbone effect.

promises to wear almost indefinitely; the design and color express Mrs. Borsodi's personality. What more could be expected of any garment than that it should be attractive, useful, inexpensive, and that its production should furnish a creative outlet for the artistic abilities of its maker?

To me the part which our loom and sewing-machine have played in creative living is, if anything, more important than the service they have rendered in making us less dependent upon earning money.

Chapter Five - Shelter

FOR many years, shelter for us had meant the four walls of an apartment in New York City with all the conveniences and services which were included in the rent we paid. We took electricity and gas, running hot and cold water, steam heat and modern plumbing, and janitor service, quite for granted. It is true that a few years before our flight from the city we had moved into a house in Flushing, a half-hour from the center of the city. We then made the discovery that it was possible for us to run a house and that we could have much more room, for the same rent, if we were willing to burden ourselves with the responsibility for producing our own hot water and our own heat in the winter. This experience helped to get us into a frame of mind in which we could seriously consider living in a house in the country in which there were none of the comforts to which we were accustomed, until we installed them and maintained them for ourselves. The purchase of a home in which they were already present was out of question because our funds were too small, and besides, that would have reduced the field in which we might experiment with building and making things for ourselves.

The house on the place which we purchased when we moved to the country twelve years ago--our present home is not on the same place--was in part very old. Hewn timbers, fitted together with wooden pins, had been used in the construction of one part of the building. The newer section must have been added many years later, since the timbers were regulation stuff. In addition, this new section must have at one time been a separate building, because the ceilings in the two sections were of different heights with the floor levels of the second story varying correspondingly. The entrance was at one side of the house and the front door decorated with a stupid little porch. Study of the lines of the building led us to the conclusion that the door would have to be shifted to the center and the window in the center moved to where the door was. The front porch, we decided, was an anachronism which had no place in our picture of the sort of house we wanted. At the back was a door which for some unknown reason opened into the thin air with a sheer drop of three feet to the ground. There were partitions inside where openings should have been, and doors had been cut where there should have been solid walls.

There was no electricity, no gas, no bathroom, no heating system. There wasn't even a fireplace, something for which we had romantically hungered. The only thing approaching a convenience was an old-fashioned hand suction pump in the kitchen connected to an iron sink. But we found out that it didn't work, and besides, that it was connected to a cistern in which there was rarely any water.

To make this house over into what would furnish us the equivalent of the comforts to which we were accustomed would have required the employment of carpenters, of joiners, of plasterers, of plumbers, of steam-fitters, of electricians.

To us these necessary alterations loomed up portentously. If the house was to be made livable, all of them would have to be made, and since we lacked the means to employ contractors to make all of them for us, there was only one way out of the dilemma, and that was to undertake to make most of them myself. An initial experience with contractors helped to strengthen our determination in this direction. We had purchased an electric range--price $75—for use in the country. We made arrangements with an electrician to install the range the day after we arrived, and received a bill for $35 for the work--nearly half the cost of the range. Whether the charge was exorbitant or not, it seemed to us high, and to me it did not seem to involve much in the way of skills which I could not master.

I began to accumulate tools from that moment, and decided to train myself for the job of jack-of-all-trades by undertaking to build something on which my 'prentice could do no irretrievable damage. A new chicken-house was elected. The shanty we had found on the place, and which had been used for a chicken- house, was such a dirty, hopelessly inefficient mess that it had to be torn down. With what could be retrieved from the lumber in the old chicken-house and a few new two-by-fours and boards, I began to build a chicken-house.

The building of that chicken-house proved a liberal education. If it did not make me into a finished carpenter, it at least gave me the courage to under-take the remodeling of the house, and eventually make it over to something nearer to our idea of what a modest country home should look like.

In the course of the year during which I spent all my spare hours remodel-ing the house, building in cupboards and closets and furniture, putting in electric lights, installing an automatic pumping system, I acquired a whole-some confidence in my ability to work with tools. I learned that deficiencies of experience and skill could be offset by the time and pains put into each job. Before I was through with my building operations on "Sevenacres,"I came to the conclusion that most of the work which we think only skilled mechanics can do is quite within the capacities of any intelligent and perse-vering man. While some of the work which they do, and certainly the speed with which they can work, requires years of experience, most of their skills involve relatively simple techniques. The mysterious knowledge which makes the average city man, in his ignorance, telephone for an electrician whenever a fuse blows out or an electric light fixture fails to function, and to hunt for the janitor or call for a plumber when a faucet leaks, hasn't the right to be mysterious to anyone over the age of fifteen.

The effort to produce shelter for ourselves in this way produced a number of dividends upon which we had not counted in the beginning. We, of course, counted most upon reducing the cost of shelter. In the city, a full quarter of our income had been spent for rent. By owning our home, and above all by making our investment small because we were willing to put some of our own labor into rebuilding, we cut down the cost of shelter to not much more than I earned by one or two days' work a month. That left just so much more of what we used to spend for rent available for other purposes than shelter; we had the income for from four to five days more each month to save or spend.

One of the dividends upon which we had not counted was that of health. We found that this sort of work, if it was not overdone (of which there is a real danger when one's enthusiasm is great), furnishes wholesome and nec-essary exercise. And instead of being just the mechanical exercise of gymna-sium work, it is exercise for the intellect and the emotions as well.

Another dividend was the discovery that building could be fun. Slowly but surely the things we conceived first as an idea finally became realities em-bodied in sticks and stones. The space where we decided that a cupboard was needed was eventually occupied by one, and the cupboard we dreamed and designed on a piece of paper eventually grew into a real cupboard which served a functional purpose in our lives. The satisfaction of standing off and looking at it when the last stroke of the paint-brush had been laid upon it was emotionally much the same thing felt by an artist when surveying a painting which he had finally finished. The creative artist and the creative carpenter are brothers under the skin. Creating and making things has its pains, no doubt, but it has pleasures so great that they offset the pains.

One dividend upon which we had not counted was the discovery that the right kind of machines often made up for the lack of skill--and the lack of strength--of an inexperienced craftsman such as myself. A concrete-mixer can furnish the strength for mixing sand and stone and cement to a man who ordinarily never does any work heavier than shoving a pen across the papers on a desk. And an electric saw can furnish him the skill to make a square and plumb cut on a rafter which he might never be able to acquire with a hand saw.

Out of this discovery grew our workshop, equipped with all sorts of power-driven machines which furnished skill, supplied strength, and saved labor. In spite of the fact that in my case I had to start with zero in the way of experience in buying tools and machines, most of the purchases made for the shop have proved to be paying investments. I use the term workshop symbolically rather than geographically, for many kinds of work are done and many of our tools are kept outside of the workshop itself. Our shop now includes

"Dogwoods," the main house on the homestead. One of the wings contains the workshop, the other, the loom room. Designed and built by amateur labor. Even the wiring, plumbing, and steam fitting were done by what can at best be described as semi-skilled labor. The stonework in all the houses on "Dogwoods" was put in by amateurs, using a modification of the Flagg Method of wall-building.

equipment for building with stone and cement, for carpentry, for plumbing and steam fitting, for electrical wiring, for painting, and for heavier work such as hauling, grading and excavating, pulling stumps, and even blasting. We ought to have, but haven't as yet, a forge and a lathe. When we install these machines for metal-working we shall be able to do almost any job which may develop in connection with the running and development of our homestead.

This equipment wasn't all purchased at once. It was acquired piece by piece as necessity dictated and as our purse permitted. I never, however, hesitated to buy a piece of machinery on credit or installments if I felt confident that it would pay for itself eventually out of its savings. The concrete-mixer, for instance, was purchased when we decided to build our new home of stone instead of wood. It has been used not only to build one house, but four houses, and the last considerable job for which it was used was the mixing of the concrete for our swimming-pool. This was built almost wholly by our two boys, and but for this piece of machinery and the tractor and scraper used in excavating the ground, it would have been an impossible task for them. The mixer has paid for itself over and over again, and it still stands, old and battered, it is true, but ready for the same sort of service it has furnished us in the past.

Another piece of machinery which served in many different ways was a combination circular saw, planing-machine, and drill. These combination machines are, on the basis of my experience, a mistake. Separate machines are better in the long run, even though the investment in them is somewhat greater. We have used the drill on this combination hardly at all, and a separate band saw and separate planing-machine would be better than the machine which we purchased. The band saw can handle heavy timber as well as ordinary lumber, timbers for which the circular saw is too small. Nevertheless we have used our saw machine on many jobs, though it is now relegated mainly to the job of cutting wood for our fireplaces and kitchen stove. Recently we managed to rig up an attachment which enabled us to use a much larger saw on this machine, and we have discovered that it is possible for us to rip boards up to six inches in width out of logs grown in our own woodlot. In our section of the country the blight has killed all the chestnut trees, and we have quantities of this fine hardwood which we were burning until it occurred to me that we might use this chestnut for making furniture. By this coming winter we shall have accumulated a quantity of chestnut lumber and shall then turn in earnest to furniture-making.

Our circular-saw machine was supplemented after a time with an electric hand saw--one of the most useful tools on our place. It has proved not only a great time and muscle saver, but has added immensely to the skill of everyone who has used it. It takes a skilled carpenter to make a perfectly square cut with a hand saw. The electric saw makes it possible for any handy man to do an extremely workman-like job. And of course when it comes to ripping boards, the speed with which it does the work delights the heart.

An equally useful tool has been our electric hand drill. It has, for one thing, almost relegated the brace and bit to limbo. We never use so slow a tool except for holes too large for our electric drill. We use this tool not only for drilling in wood and iron, but also for reaming pipes, and sometimes for sharpening tools. We have other machines which are not quite so often used--a sander, and a paint-machine, for example. As all our houses are built of stone, we do not have much painting of large surfaces with which to bother, so we have not the need of a painting machine which those who build of wood would have. Taking them as a whole, these machines have made it possible for us to build up our place steadily, and to add improvements during odd times which would otherwise be wasted. It is largely because of these machines that we have built four stone houses on our places--three residences and a stone barn.

Our determination to build in stone dates back to discovery of Ernest Flagg's experiments in the building of attractive and economical small houses. Flagg developed a system of building out of stone and concrete, using forms in which to lay the walls, which greatly reduced the cost of stone construction. Relatively unskilled labor could build Flagg walls which were attractive, which were sound, and which were true. As a result, we found ourselves building of stone--the natural building material for a county with the name Rockland—at a cost not much higher than that of good frame construction.

My enthusiasm for many of Flagg's ideas has not abated. For instance, he calls attention to the absurdity of cellars under houses built in the country. The cellar usually represents a fifth of the cost of the house. For much less money, the storage space ordinarily furnished by a cellar can be provided by adding to the area of the building. Except where the contour of the ground calls for a basement or cellar, all our houses are built on what are virtually concrete platforms, over which the regular floors have been laid.

Another idea of his has been the building of one-story houses, without attics and with low walls, using dormers over doors and windows to secure height where height is needed. This makes it possible to build outside stone walls which are not more than four or five feet in height for the most part, so that stone and concrete do not have to be carried up to a considerable height and scaffolds erected on which to work. The use of what he calls ridge dormers or ridge skylights makes it easy to ventilate these one-story houses in summer.

But one of the things most attractive to me in Flagg's type of construction is the number of designs which can be built around courts, section by section. This makes it possible to build a part of a house to begin with, and add to it as means permit. When we started to build our main house on the new place, we first finished one wing of the house, and lived in it until the main part was finished. That took us over a year. The whole house is not even now finished--nor do I see any reason why it should ever be. A home, it seems to me, should grow like the human beings it shelters. Building one's shelter in this way, section by section, made it much easier for us to finance the building of the sort of home to which we aspired. And it should make it very much easier for those who have not enough money at the beginning for all the home that their vision paints for them.

Chapter Six - Water, Hot Water, and Waste Water

THE great adventure, on which we had embarked when we left the city, did not contemplate any return to primitive ways of life.

We had no intentions of going in for manual labor just for the sweet discipline of hard work. We had no intention, therefore, of being satisfied with drawing water hand over hand from a well--a laborious form of drudgery still prevailing on many of the farms of the country. And certainly we had no romantic notions about carrying water from a flowing brook-- good enough fora camping trip, but ridiculous as a permanent way of living. We were not after any such return to nature. What we wanted were all the comforts of the city in addition to the comforts which country life had to offer. There would be enough hard work, we knew, without making a virtue of doing things the hardest way.

The water supply on "Sevenacres" when we purchased it came from a well about twenty-five feet from the kitchen door, and from a cistern fed by rain water from the eve troughs of the house. Water was drawn from the well by two oak buckets on chains which were pulled up over a pulley. A suction pump in the kitchen was supposed to draw water from the cistern. This pump was out of order, but after being repaired, in the course of which we all received our first lesson in applied hydraulics, we discovered that this was a most uncertain source of water, since the cistern was too small to carry a supply between most spells of wet weather. So we installed an automatic electric pumping system--an outfit which at that time represented an investment of $125, but which can now be purchased for around $50. With the services of a plumber to connect it up, an expenditure of $150 put running water into the house.

What did it cost us for water? Did it cost us more than in the city, where we had the benefits of mass pumping and mass distribution through water mains? On "Sevenacres" I had no occasion to work out this problem, but when we dug our well and installed our pumping system on the "Dogwoods," I decided to find out, and kept records, so that at the end of a number of years I would be in position to answer the question with some degree of accuracy.

Some years after we were living in our new home I had quite an argument with my friend, Ralph W. Hench, who lives in Suffern, upon this point. The Hench family, of course, enjoyed the luxury of city water. Water cost them, he told me, $20 per year. And he was quite certain that mine cost me much more than that. There was no man better equipped than Hench with whom to argue the point, since he was in charge of the accounting for one of the largest corporations of the country, and the question could only be correctly answered if approached from an accounting standpoint.

We made a detailed calculation of what it had cost us to supply ourselves with water on the "Dogwoods" during the seven years we had lived there. The capital investment in our system was as follows:

Cost of well.................................$170
Complete pumping outfit.............150
Labor...20
Total Amount..............................$340

The labor costs are, if anything, high, since I was my own contractor and only unskilled labor was used. These figures are too high according to present-day price levels. Our outfit can probably be duplicated for a third less than it cost us. Not only have prices come down owing to the depression, but technological advances in pump manufacture, motors, tanks, fittings, etc., have brought down costs materially.

We then projected costs upon an annual basis as follows:

Interest on capital of $340 at 6 per cent..$20.40
Depreciation on pumping system at 5 per cent of $170............................8.50
Repairs per year covering seven years...4.29
Electric current..12.00
Annual cost of water..$45.19

The moment we had these figures my friend exclaimed: "There you are--it is costing you over twice as much as it costs me in Suffern."

I went to the telephone and called up a mutual acquaintance who we both agreed was the best judge of realty values in Suffern, and asked him this question: "Suppose there were two lots for sale in Suffern, both of them equally desirable in every respect except one. Suppose one of them was located on the Suffern water system, and suppose the other was located where no water could be supplied to the owner by the city. What would the difference in the price of the two lots be?"

After considering the matter a moment, he replied, "About $500--perhaps a little more or a little less." Then I started out to figure what it cost my friend Wench for water in Suffern. And these were the figures at which we finally agreed:

Interest on capital investment of $500 at 6 per cent............................$30.00
Taxes on added land value--3-1/5 per cent of the $250 assessment.......8.00
Water tax..20.00
Annual cost of water..$58.00

This showed a clear saving of $12.81per year in favor of the individual pumping system. "But I am not through yet," I said. "This figure of $58," I went on, "represents what it costs for water in Suffern on a single lot. But many homes in Suffern are built upon two or more lots, thus doubling the initial investment, and correspondingly raising the hidden cost of securing water from the city mains. While if there were eighteen acres of land around a home, as there is around mine, the cost of water would be prohibitive for any but the wealthiest of families."

Here with regard to water we have another of the many illustrations available of the mistaken idea that mass production is of necessity economical. With water, as with other conveniences and with most products, what is saved by mass production tends to be lost in the costs of distribution. It undoubtedly costs the city of Suffern less to pump water than it costs me in the country. My small and relatively inefficient pumping system cannot hope to compete in cost per gallon of water raised with the large and relatively efficient pumping system of a city of many thousands of people. But when I pump my water on the "Dogwoods," all costs in connection with water end. When the city pumps its water, its real costs of supplying water only begin. It is the cost of distributing the water through an expensive system of water-mains which absorbs the economies of the "mass" pumping, and replaces them with an actual higher cost than that of the individual homesteader The city's investment and operating costs for its pumping system are negligible in comparison with its investment and maintenance costs for its water mains. The pumping costs are taken care of by the water tax, but the distribution costs are hidden in higher land values, except right when the mains are laid when they are made visible in the form of assessments against the lots before which they have been laid.

What is true of water is true of many of the public services which are enjoyed by those living in cities today. Just as mains are laid to distribute water, sewers are laid to assemble waste water. The two functioned for us in the city without our being hardly conscious of the fact. If we were to be equally comfortable in the country, we would have to solve the waste-water problem as we had that of running water.

A decent sewage-disposal system is unquestionably one of the essentials of a civilized existence. I can see nothing charming in the way in which this problem is handled by savages in a so-called state of nature, and the way in which it is handled in most country homes today, with uncomfortable and sometimes unsanitary outhouses, seems to me but little better. When we began to study this problem, we found, as we had with so many others, that the benefits of a modern sewage-disposal system could be enjoyed in the country without the expense of paying for maintaining the sewers and sewage-disposal plants for the operation of which city dwellers pay such an unconscionable sum. Looked at from its broadest standpoint, the system generally used today involves a shocking waste of the nation's soil resources. It is no exaggeration of the actual situation to say that we are now taking up organic material from the soil, converting it into foodstuffs, and then destroying that organic matter irretrievably with fire and chemicals in these wage disposal plants of our cities.

In studying this problem, we became aware of the fact that we had, in common with others who enjoyed the benefits of city life, paid for sewage disposal even though we had been unaware of the fact. Unless the city man happens to own his own home--and the vast majority do not—he has no direct knowledge of what taxes are paid for. All he knows is that he pays rent. The fact that part of his rent really pays for running water, for sewage, garbage and ash disposal, is hardly realized by him, just as when he lives in an apartment he forgets that another substantial part of his rent really pays for heat, hot water, janitor service and all the conveniences of his apartment. What we discovered was that we could have practically every service of this sort essential to our comfort, without having to pay a premium price for them.

A simple and inexpensive septic tank, with a drainage tile system to dispose of the overflow from the tank, is all that is needed in order not only to dodge the heavy cost of sewage disposal in the city, but for converting the waste into a contribution to soil fertility. What is taken from the soil is then returned. After we installed such a system on our place in the country, the sewage problem vanished for us.

Hot water, and plenty of it, is necessary to comfort by present standards of living. In the apartment houses in which we used to live we secured our supply from the hot-water taps in seemingly unlimited quantities. We were determined to solve the problem of producing it for ourselves with practically no labor and at a lower cost than we had paid for it in the city--concealed inside the rent we had paid each month.

It is almost impossible to be clean without a plentiful supply of really hot water. For dish-washing, water which is merely lukewarm is an irritation rather than a comfort. Yet in spite of the fact that plenty of hot water is essential to comfort, millions of homes in America still depend upon such primitive methods as teakettles and side-arm-stove heaters for their supply of hot water.

The teakettle, we found, furnishes some really hot water, if the fire under it is always a brisk one. But the quantity which can be heated is hardly enough for the needs of the kitchen alone. And of course it requires dozens of trips back and forth filling the teakettle with water and emptying the hot water into the vessel in which it is to be used. The labor and strength involved in making these trips may seem trifling, but repeated dozens of times daily, it totals up to a surprising amount of time and a considerable amount of fatigue, for neither of which there is any real necessity. Modern offices and factories are efficient just in proportion to the extent to which they eliminate all such wastes of time and strength. There is no reason why our homes should be run at lower standards of efficiency. And such efficiency pays in dollars as well as in happiness.

Every bit of time and strength saved from unnecessary labor--especially non-creative labor such as that involved in cleaning, carrying water, washing, and similar work--frees an equivalent amount of time and strength for productive and creative work. Some of Mrs. Borsodi's friends wonder how she, even with the assistance of servants, gets the time to do the quantities of cooking, baking, preserving, sewing, and even weaving which go on in her home. By using labor-saving appliances and machines to eliminate as much non-productive work as possible, time is saved which can be used to produce these things. An investment in an efficient water-heating system, for instance, which eliminates the non-productive work of carrying water back and forth, pays for itself over and over again by what it enables the family to save in making things which it would otherwise have to buy. It is for this reason that the teakettle method of producing hot water seems to us as obsolete as the Dutch oven. It doesn't pay. It not only is unequal to the requirements for hot water in bathing; it makes a supplementary method of heating absolutely essential for laundering. And we have found doing our own laundry at home is one of the easiest ways in which to pay for an efficient system of hot-water heating.

We started to get away from the tyranny of the teakettle with a small coal heater in the cellar. Water was piped from it to a storage tank, and from the tank to the various hot-water faucets. This was an inexpensive installation, and furnished a good supply of hot water without too much expense. The fire, however, had to be attended to several times each day, and the ashes carried out periodically.

In an effort to get rid of this labor we installed a kerosene heater. The first one we tried out was wickless. Our kerosene was evidently not clear enough for this type of heater, and the burners frequently crusted, thus interfering with its efficiency as well as creating an unpleasant cleaning job. True, we had a plentiful supply of hot water; the cost, however, was a little higher than coal, and we still had the unpleasant chore of filling the oil-reservoir daily and cleaning the heater occasionally.

Next we tried a kerosene heater with wicks. This proved an improvement in one respect only--if we changed the wicks frequently enough we avoided the unpleasant cleaning job with which we had to struggle before. We still had the daily filling of the oil-tank on our hands--so the job was still by no means automatic.

Finally we decided to go in for a completely automatic installation. A very low rate permitted us to install an electric heater on an off-peak rate. Where the power company has established such a rate, this type of heater is economical and efficient, and it requires no attention whatever. The off-peak rate is still a new idea; in many cases completely automatic hot water can be most inexpensively secured with gas. In country homes not reached by the mains of a gas company, portable gas-tanks can be used and while the cost is higher, itis still, in our judgment, not so different from ordinary gas as to warrant some of the methods which we discarded.

Our experiments with the various methods of heating water, as with other domestic appliances, have thoroughly convinced us that the investment and cost of maintaining the most efficient means for furnishing the home with utilities and comforts are quite within the income limitations of most families in this country. It may not be possible to install all of these comforts in the very beginning, any more than we were able to, but they are distinctly economical if the time which they save is used for productive work in reducing and eliminating butcher, baker, grocer, and clothier bills.

Chapter Seven - Education--The School of Living

WHEN we were considering shaking the dust of the city from our feet, the school question was one which caused us a great deal of worry. Our boys were seven and eight years old; they had been going to school from the time they had entered the kindergarten classes in the city's public schools. At the time we were planning to leave the city they had already made more scholastic progress than other children of their age; one was a half-year ahead, and the other a full year ahead, of their chronological age. The credit for this, we now know, was due less to the elaborately organized public schools of New York City than to our use at home of same of the methods of child-training developed by Dr. Maria Montessori, the Italian educator, in whose theories the country was just then becoming interested. We had used the Montessori methods from the moment the boys were old enough to start feeding and dressing themselves. So impressed were we by her approach to the problem of child education that we constructed our own "didactic" apparatus because nonc of it was at that time on sale in this country.

Without having pushed our boys, but merely by giving them a chance to take advantage of the opportunities which the schools offered them, they were making excellent progress. Now we were committing ourselves to a way of living which would take them away from the educational advantages of city schools. Should we risk what would happen to them in one of the "little red schoolhouses" which still abounded in 1920 in New York State? If we were confronted by such an emergency, would we prove equal to teaching them at home? We decided we would. When I compared Mrs. Borsodi to the average school-teacher in the public schools, I saw no reason why she could not teach the children just as well, if not better, at home. She might lack the technique for handling a large class, and she might not have been drilled in the syllabus required by the state Board of Regents, but when it came to individual instruction, I was confident that she could do more for the children than could public schools, no matter how well managed.

When we finally got to the country, our worst expectations were realized. The school in our district was impossible. The school board consisted of "old-timers" whose principal concern was to keep the tax rate down. Not only were the teachers which the board selected unequal to their responsibilities, but the social and moral atmosphere was bad. In that respect it was worse than the city. There at least the contacts of our boys with children whom we considered undesirable were limited. And the number of children made it possible to select only those for companionship of whom we approved. In a small school, such as that with which we had to contend, the damage which the bullies or perverts are able to do is all out of proportion to the damage which they can do in a large one. The situation in our district, and I believe in the country generally, has in the past decade shown great improvement. The coming of the school bus has made it possible to eliminate most of the impoverished one-room schools, and in the large consolidated schools which have taken their place, city conditions of school organization are to a large extent duplicated.

We first tried cooperation with the school board and with the teachers. Most of the board members proved impossible. When we talked about educational problems to them, we found ourselves talking in a foreign tongue. The teachers were, in general, not quite so hopeless; at least they knew what we were talking about. But most of them were immature; most of them had been more or less ruined by the rigid regimentation which the state required of them. We did manage to win the cooperation of the first teacher to whom the boys were turned over, and as long as she was in charge of the school she tried to make the conventional scheme work. But the next teacher resented bitterly our interest, and reluctantly we decided that this method of trying to make the country school endurable was love's labor lost.

We finally decided to take the boys out of school altogether.

A talk with the county superintendent of education won his cooperation. In fact, he decided that the sort of education our boys would receive under the plan we outlined would more than meet the requirements of the law. Our plan was to use the regular textbooks, to follow the state procedure in teaching as laid down in the syllabus of each subject, and to have one of the public-school teachers who lived in the neighborhood come in once each month to put the boys through an examination which would insure their finishing up each year precisely as well as did the boys attending public school. This plan, we believed, would prepare them for high-school even though they had none of the "benefits" of classwork for a few years.

Thus began our experiment in domestic education. And again, individual production proved its superiority to mass production. Mrs. Borsodi found it possible to give the boys, in two hours' desk work, all the training which they were supposed to get, according to the state, in a whole school day plus the work which they were supposed to do at home. One of her first discoveries was that the training of the boys on such sheer fundamentals as addition, subtraction, multiplication, and division had been so poor that mathematical progress and understanding were almost impossible. She made the boys retrace their steps. Some conscientious drilling on the A, B, Cs, and they were then able to gallop through the more difficult parts of arithmetic. Working closely with them, she knew whether or not they really understood. She did not have to rely upon an examination to find out--an examination which revealed little to the teacher because of its mechanical limitations. Two hours of such study, I agreed with Mrs. Borsodi, were sufficient for the sort of thing upon which the public schools concentrated; the rest of the day would prove of more educational value to the boys if devoted to reading and play. The play, in such a home, was just as educational as the reading. Productive and creative activities in the garden, the kitchen, the workshop, the loom-room furnished the boys opportunities to "play" in ways since adopted as regular procedure by the progressive schools. In our home, however, such play was directly related to useful functions; they were not merely interesting exercises.

Best of all, the new scheme furnished plenty of time for reading. The reading seemed to us all important. One of the terrible things which the average school does to its pupils is to kill their love for books. All books, to the child who has had to "read" in class, tend to become textbooks. The poetry, plays, novels, essays which are parts of their courses in English are read, not to furnish rich experiences and to expand the imagination, but as subjects for recitation and grammatical analysis. This is a process which dissects what should be a living thing, and the corpse of a poem which the child is made to study is no more what the artists who created it intended it to be than the corpse which medical students dissect is a living, breathing human being. The reading of Ivanhoe was a part of the prescribed course of English in the public school during the years they attended the district school. They were required to read in class a paragraph at a time daily. The idea horrified me. So I suggested that they read the whole story through at home without regard to their class work. The result more than pleased me. The boys discovered that Ivanhoe was a fascinating story; one of them read it through several times before tiring of it. Instead of hating the story, they learned to love it.

As a result of our insistence upon the fact that reading was fun, rather than work, books came to play naturally the part in their lives which they should play in every educated person's existence. Their imaginations were broadened; the provincialism of city and country so prevalent today became impossible to them; even the textbooks acquired, by sympathetic magic, an entirely different significance from that which they develop in schools. Instead of consisting of lessons to be memorized in preparation for "exams," they were found to be keys to the accumulated knowledge of mankind. We found, however, that the Encyclopaedia Britannica was better for this purpose than all their textbooks put together.

Most parents will probably shrink from considering such an undertaking because of the amount of time they believe they would have to devote to it. But such a supposition is a mistaken one. It really does not take much time. We have acquired our notions about the number of hours children should study daily from the amount of time which they usually spend in school. There is a dreary waste of time inescapable in the process of mass education. Most of the time of the children in public schools is devoted to waiting, not studying. Studying of a sort is prescribed as a means of filling in the time devoted to waiting. The children wait in classes, and they wait between classes. Occasionally there is an educational contact between teacher and pupil. In between these contacts, the children are kept out of mischief by an amazingly ingenious series of time-filling exercises. What I consider an educational contact is usually a fortunate accident in our conventional schools. Education is the exception, not the rule, because only when a child feels a need for information and explanation, and feels it emotionally and intellectually and not mechanically, is that educational contact established. Mostly when these needs develop in the lives of school children, the routine of the schoolroom prevents the teacher from responding to it, and the hunger is dissipated and replaced by boredom.

Our experience showed that in such a home as we were establishing these opportunities abounded. Education was really reciprocal; in the very effort to educate the boys, we educated ourselves. Indeed, it is a notion of mine that no real educational influence is exerted upon the pupil unless there is also an incidental educational effect upon the teacher. The average public school is operated upon the theory that this personal relationship is unwise; that the relationship should be impersonal, objective, and mechanical, the example of Socrates and the peripatetic school to the contrary notwithstanding.

With our method, we not only managed to avoid the handicap of a poor school, but the whole Borsodi family seemed to be going to school. But it proved to be a school so different from that to which most of us have become accustomed that I have had to invent a special name for it—the school of living.

In this school the members of the family, old and young, and those who have lived with us, have been both faculty and students. The subject which they studied has been *living,* the pedagogic system has been what might be called the *work-play* method, the textbooks have been anything and everything printed which touched upon the problems of the good life in any way. The absence of formality in this school may deceive the uninitiated, and the fact that a systematic educational activity is going forward may be overlooked. For that reason I once put down the various projects which have in one way or another been the subjects of our study, and found that they formed a fairly comprehensive curriculum falling into four major divisions-- Art and Science, Management, History, Philosophy.

Philosophy is a subject remote and distant from life as it comes to most people in school. Yet there is no reason why it should be. We need desperately philosophy as a guide to life. We need it as a tool with which to train thought--logic for everyday use. But we need it also to form values and habits. We need for every-day living (1) economic policies, (2) physiological, (3) social, (4) biological, (5) psychological habits; and (6) religious, (7) moral, (8) political (9) educational, (10) individual values. Why should we not approach the practical questions which fall under these various academic classifications from a philosophic point of view? Yet as a matter of fact we make most of our decisions—or acceptances of decisions made by others--with utter disregard of their philosophic implications.

History is another subject which undergoes a transformation when it too is domesticated. History really has three aspects with us: (1) past--which is the aspect to which it is usually confined; (2) current history—to which the schools have only in recent years awakened; and (3) future history, which is to me most important of all. We have to make plans, we have to adopt policies, we have to determine values--but these cannot be formulated wisely unless one projects past and present into the future. Yet there is scarcely a day in our lives when such planning might not be made to add immensely to our comfort and happiness if it were approached from a historical standpoint.

Art and science--sundered by the specialists into whose care their study has been intrusted by our schools--need to be brought together in selecting and preparing food, in designing clothes and costumes, in building and furnishing our homes. We need more chemists in our kitchens, and fewer in our laboratories; just as we need more artists in them and fewer in our large advertising agencies. Every single step in practical living has both its artistic and its scientific aspects, and we do not live richly unless we bring to bear upon these apparently humble and yet all-important living problems all the accumulated wisdom and skill of the ages.

Finally, we need to study management—the management of living, not of business. We have management problems as individuals, as families, as civic groups--why should we not apply to home problems the care and thought and attention which we now bestow upon production, purchasing, marketing, and finance in business? Every family has to finance itself; every family has purchasing of many kinds to carry on--and how poorly that is done only those familiar with Consumers' Research can realize; every family markets services or produce, and practically every family produces more or less in its kitchens, sewing-rooms, gardens. Under the scheme of living with which we have been experimenting, domestic and individual production becomes so immeasurably more important, that study of it is essential if it is to be efficiently carried on.

Here are most of the subjects taught in our schools and universities, but in a new guise. As we have studied them they are not subjects so much as essential parts of the whole problem of living. In the schools, specialization and the division of labor among the teachers, and preparation for a life of specialization and the division of labor among the students, has led to the isolation of each particular subject. In the intense concentration upon each narrow field, the relationship of each subject to life as a whole is distorted and the true significance of what is studied is obscured. We ought, for instance, to study chemistry in order that we may live more richly; instead, we live in order to develop and promote and expand chemical activity and chemical industry. Means and ends are thus reversed, just as in our factories today men and women take it quite for granted that it is sane to devote their lives to the production of something to be sold or marketed, instead of devoting the best part of each day to the creation or production of something which enriches their own lives.

In nothing is the present-day mistakes of educational institutions more apparent to me than in the separation of art and science into separate, air-tight, and mutually opposed specialities. We have not only separate teachers and separate courses--we have separate schools for the arts and for the sciences, with not a little contempt on the part of each group for those devoting themselves to the other. As a result, we are busily producing artists who are ignorant of science, and engineers who are ignorant of art. If beauty and richness be considered the ends and objects of living, and the scientific and engineering techniques the means for attaining this end, then we are actually producing painters, writers, sculptors, poets who are supposed to specialize on the ends or objects of living, and scientists, engineers, chemists who are taught the means but not the ends to be attained. The result is a sterile art, divorced from life, and a meaningless multiplication of sky-scrapers, subways, sewers, dams, bridges, and engineering works of all kinds.

In the homely things of life, so important in the aggregate, this separation of art and science is now almost universal. For instance, take such a homely thing as bread--the staff of life. Bread ought to be nutritious and it ought to be tasty. One without the other is an absurdity. Yet we have chemists in our universities studying bread scientifically. They produce all sorts of facts about vitamins, about fermentation, about nutrition. And then we have, even today, many housewives baking bread and governing their approach to the problem primarily by taste. The one sees bread as an object, scientifically; the other sees it as a flavor much as might an artist. Because of the housewife's ignorance of science, she may ruin her family's health; because of the scientist's ignorance of art, bread is produced which is unfit for consumption by cultivated palates. Of the two, the scientist may actually do more harm than the housewife, though it is hard to be certain about the matter. At least the housewife's bread may taste well and so add to the pleasures of the table, but the scientist may reduce eating to the level of stoking a boiler.

Some day I hope a group of intelligent and cultured people may find it worth while to establish such a school of living. Such a school, if it included enough families to determine really what is the good life experimentally, would furnish a demonstration of how to live to which the whole world might listen. Such a group would demonstrate that it is possible for men and women to make themselves independent and economically secure, and that centering educational activities directly upon the problems of living would add immeasurably to mankind's happiness and comfort.

The world is badly in need of such a demonstration. All that the Borsodi family has thus far managed to do has been to show how badly it is needed.

Chapter Eight - Capital

JUST what to say about the capital needed to establish a homestead is one of the most difficult matters with which I find that I have undertaken to grapple. Yet it is one question about which I am asked more frequently than almost any other by those who express a liking for the way of living with which the Borsodi family has been experimenting. Before attempting to deal with the matter, however, I think it important to dispel an illusion under which many people who have heard about our experiment seem to labor. Typical of these people is one man, connected with one of our agricultural schools, who assumed that because the houses, land, machinery, and livestock comprising our homestead represented an investment of at least $15,000 (according to his estimate), that therefore the capital with which I began the experiment must have been $15,000. "With $15,000,"he wrote me, "I would not need such a homestead in order to make myself independent. Invested in stocks and bonds, that sum would furnish a comfortable living without going to all the trouble of producing everything for one's own use on a small farm. For most people who desire independence and security the problem is how to get the$15,000 not what to do with it after they get it."

It is an interesting commentary upon the tenacity with which even intelligent people maintain conventional illusions that such a letter was written to me after the collapse of the securities market in 1929.In spite of the collapse of the houses of cards which buyers of securities everywhere were discovering they had erected for themselves, this man still believed that dependence upon investments in stocks and bonds was superior to dependence upon a homestead equipped with livestock, tools, and machinery with which a family could produce a plentiful living for themselves no matter what happened to the business world. If the depression should have taught him anything, it should have made him see that stocks and bonds furnish no one real security. The only possible security in our present chaos is direct access to the opportunity to produce for oneself the essentials of a comfortable living.

But even if it were true, as my friendly critic believed, that there were such things as *secure* securities, the point remains that in the beginning there was no $15,000 invested in the Borsodi homestead. Certainly I was never confronted with the alternative of investing $15,000 in stocks and bonds or of investing it in a homestead. Yet it is true that today, after twelve years of slow growth, the homestead does represent a large investment, an investment much greater than the sum at which this critic valued it. It is the way in which we started out to live, not the fact that we had the capital before we left the city, which explains our possession today of a fairly well-equipped home. If one can lay hands upon just enough with which to start, then a $15,000 homestead should come ultimately by the sheer development which such a way of living makes possible.

The question, therefore, is not how to secure $15,000, but how to secure enough with which to start. And enough with which to start can be saved by many families, I maintain, in spite of the inequalities and injustices of our present social system. How much, then, is really needed in the beginning? That depends in most cases on two things: what sort of income from "jobs" the family can depend upon while it is establishing itself, and how much it is willing to endure in the way of hardships for the first year or two. If the income is an average "white collar" salary, hardships can be quickly eliminated. If the income is very much smaller, the original investment must be larger or the family must be willing to endure a rather Spartan regime until the equipment for producing the comforts of country life is gradually purchased. Our own experience illustrates the principles involved.

When we left the city, we had as capital only the small savings which we had managed to accumulate in spite of the "accidents" which periodically prevent savings accounts from growing as they theoretically should. In addition, I had a salary of $50 per week --not a very high one for the post-war period. We purchased a place for $4,000, paying down $500, and arranged to pay off the balance in monthly installments of $50. This was smaller than the rent of $65 we had been accustomed to pay in the city even when interest and taxes are included. After paying for our place we found ourselves with hardly enough cash on hand to move and get settled in the new place. We did invest $75 in the electric range. But all purchases of livestock, of tools, of labor-saving comforts, had to come out of income. Two things, however, made that income go farther in equipping the homestead than might at first be anticipated. One was that since we spent less than we had in the city for rent and for food, even the first year, we had more money with which to make investments in equipment than we would ordinarily have saved out of salary. The other was that the investments in the more expensive equipment could be made on the installment plan. One month, for instance, we made all the purchases for our poultry-yard--incubator, eggs and setting hens. The next month we purchased our steam pressure cooker--which cost $25 at that time. Such purchases we made for cash out of what we saved from week to week. When it came to installing our automatic pumping system--an investment which ran into hundreds of dollars--we purchased it on the installment plan and had the satisfaction of seeing it save us enough to pay for itself month by month.

Yet in spite of the relatively small initial investment and the modest income in the beginning, and in spite of periods of no income or little income after I quit my job to write my first book, the homestead grew steadily and came more and more to represent that large investment which so chilled my skeptical critic. Eventually income began to go up as I cut down the time I devoted to earning money, or perhaps it would be more accurate to say I was able to secure more for my time as I became less and less dependent upon those to whom I sold my services. That made the development of the place just that much easier, and made it possible for us to start building the "Dogwoods" and to equip it as experience had taught us such a homestead should be equipped. This possibility of earning more, by needing to work less, is cumulative and is open to an immense number of professional workers. It is remarkable how much more appreciative of one's work employers and patrons become when they know that one is independent enough to decline unattractive commissions. And of course, if the wage-earning classes were generally to develop this sort of independence, employers would have to compete and bid up wages to secure workers instead of workers competing by cutting wages in order to get jobs.

That it is possible to start homesteading with even less than the Borsodi family started was demonstrated to my satisfaction by the studies I was retained to make by the Unit Committee of the Dayton, Ohio, Council of Social Agencies in connection with the establishment of homesteads for the unemployed of that city. These victims of the machine age had nothing in the way of income other than part time or odd jobs, and what they were making for their own needs through their Production Units. They had no capital at all with which to start, except the things they had managed to hang on to in the way of furniture, utensils, and personal belongings. Plans had, therefore, to be made, first to establish them on homesteads at the minimum of possible investment, and then to furnish them some sort of cash income to meet the expenses for things which they would not be able to produce for themselves. Part-time work for others in business or industry or professional life, and the sale of surplus produce, was expected to furnish an income equivalent to one or two days' work per week for at least one member of the family. With an income of between five and ten dollars per week, I estimated the homesteaders would be able to repay the advances made to them for investment in the homestead and its equipment, meet all ordinary expenditures for taxation, light, fuel, transportation, and purchase essential commodities and articles which they could not make themselves. Eventually, as their homesteads were developed they would attain a higher standard of living than that which they had previously enjoyed.

Now in determining how much was needed for the initial investment, the food to be produced--which determined the land area—was the deciding factor. A typical dietary for a middle-class family of five persons may be used as a base for this purpose, variations from it increasing or decreasing the investment. A variation toward a vegetarian diet would both decrease the land area and the investment in livestock; on the other hand, a variation toward a heavier meat diet would increase the investment in these directions. The typical diets used in the studies [1] I made for the Dayton Homestead Units was as follows:

Bread, cereals, baked goods..............................750 pounds
Vegetables and fruits..3,000 pounds
Butter, lard and other fats..................................250 pounds
Sugar, honey and other sweets..........................250 pounds
Meat and poultry..500 pounds
Eggs..200 dozen
Milk..1,200 quarts

With the exception of sugar--for which it might be possible to substitute in its entirety honey, maple sugar, and molasses—all of this food was to be produced on the proposed homesteads. Only the food items such as coffee, tea, spices, etc., would have to be purchased by the homesteaders. And of course exotic foodstuffs--oranges, pineapples, oysters, olive oil--would have to be purchased, though life could very well be maintained on whatever native foods there were which furnished the same sort of nutritive elements.

The production of 4,750 pounds of various foods, 200 dozen eggs, and the 1,200 quarts of milk above listed would require from three to five acres of land. A homestead of this size would make it possible to raise not only the food for the table, but the feed for the livestock, the livestock consisting of 25 laying hens and 25 cockerels or capons (raised from 75 chicks); two grade or pure-blooded Swiss goats with their four kids each year (two of these kids, the bucks, could be slaughtered and added to the meat diet, the does being raised and probably sold), and two hogs raised from pigs purchased each year. The bees, of which there ought to be three or four hives, would, of course, feed themselves. A considerable number of variations in this live-stock scheme are possible without materially changing the land area needed to raise feed. Turkeys, ducks, and other fowls may be added or substituted for some of the chickens; sheep raised in place of hogs; a cow used instead of milch goats. The cow would require more land than the goats; the addition of sheep or an increase in the quantity of hogs would also increase the area of land needed for grain and pasturage. The area devoted to the orchard and the kitchen garden would have to be large enough to supply about 500 quarts of vegetables and fruits to be canned and preserved for winter, or to be dehydrated if that method of food preservation is preferred.

On a three-acre homestead, about one and a half acres of the land would need to be put in grain for the goats, hogs, and chickens; about a quarter of an acre into alfalfa, soy beans or some similar crop, and a half acre reserved for pasturage. A quarter of an acre would be needed for the corn or wheat for the family's cereals. This means about two acres for field crops. The remaining acre would be all that was needed for the vegetable garden, the orchard, the barnyard, the flower-gardens and lawns, and the homesite itself. Indeed, if the family were content to live exclusively on vegetables and nuts, all its food could be raised on this one acre of land. On this general plan, three acres would be all that would be needed, while five acres would be a generous allowance. If a common pasture were made available, the three acres would be ample. I therefore suggested that the Dayton Homestead Units should consist of 160 acre tracts laid out for between thirty and thirty-five homesteads of three acres each, with the remainder of the land for common use.

Upon the basis of the land area and food program above outlined, the investment needed to establish a homestead was calculated as follows:

Land...$250
Building materials for first section of home............................300

```
Materials and equipment for other buildings............................50
Well and pump.........................................................................75
Tools and implements..............................................................25
Livestock.................................................................................75
Seeds, plants, trees, etc. .........................................................25
Sewing and loom room.............................................................75
Preserving and kitchen equipment...........................................25
Total ...................................................................................$900
```

To this investment there was added about $120 for groceries and feed for use during the first six months after movement to the land. Assuming that the homesteading started in the winter or spring, within six months production would develop to a point so that no further outside purchases would have to be made for this purpose. The total investment would therefore be around$1,000 per family. But not more than $350 to $400 of this would have to be in cash.

Farms of about 160 acres were to be laid out for the homesteads, and were to be known as Homestead Units to distinguish them from the Production Units already established by the unemployed in the city itself. In the Homestead Units the group activities and cooperative manufacturing carried on by the Production Units in the city might be continued to whatever extent the individuals in each group desired. The whole tract of land would be owned by the unit; title to the individual homesteads would be based upon perpetual leases, thus preventing speculation in land. If the farm buildings already on the tract were not suitable for use as community buildings, they would be gradually altered for this purpose. The pasture, wood lot, and community buildings would be owned by the unit as a whole and used by the individual homesteaders under rules and regulations established by the group. Tractors or horses, trucks, and heavy agricultural implements might also be cooperatively owned. Grain farming might be carried on by some units cooperatively, just as the city units produced clothes, bread, and other goods cooperatively. As much or as little communal life as the group desired was thus provided for, the balance between collectivism and individualism swinging in whatever direction experience and inclination pointed. Each family was expected, however, to build its own home, poultry-house, cow-shed, and workshop; to cultivate its own garden, and set out its own orchard and berry patch, and become in this new and modernized setting almost as self-sufficient and independent as were the pioneers of the country a hundred years ago. Trades and crafts were expected to develop and selling and bartering of produce of which individual homesteads had a surplus, but no such emphasis was to be placed upon this as to force a trend toward large-scale production.

The plans looked toward the building of permanent and beautiful homes. Construction was to follow lines developed by Ernest Flagg for the building of beautiful and inexpensive small homes. The high cost and wastes involved in building cellars was therefore to be avoided. While building the first wing of their homes, the homesteaders were to commute between Dayton and their new homes, though some of them might camp out, more or less, if the farm buildings on the site made it practicable to do so. As soon as they were on the site, they were to begin to garden, to build their own furniture in their own workshops, to weave cloth on their own looms, and to make their own clothes on their own sewing-machines. Electricity was to be brought in for both light and power, and domestic machinery and appliances used to reduce drudgery to a minimum. The crushing burdens of elaborate water and sewage systems were to be avoided by the use of individual automatic pumps and individual septic tanks.

Dayton, which is this year establishing its first homestead units, is demonstrating what can be done with very little cash even by unemployed families. But that an individual family can establish itself on a homestead with an even smaller cash investment than provided for in the Dayton plan was demonstrated to my satisfaction by a case with which I happen to be personally familiar. This family consisted of a man, wife, and boy eight years old. The man had made an indifferent living for many years as a chauffeur in and around New York, and when out of work came to live with his parents, who had a small country home in our section. One day he came to me with a project for building a road stand on a plot of land belonging to me. He had, however, no capital with which to buy the land and barely enough money to equip a stand. He asked for a lease on the lot, with the privilege of buying it if he managed to make a success of his stand. I gave him the lease for which he asked, and this is what happened:

He went to a local lumber-yard and secured a large quantity of building material on credit. With this he first built a small stand, and equipped it to sell ice cream, drinks, and the usual line of roadside refreshments. While his wife took care of the stand, he built a four-room house on the back of the lot, though the interior was unfinished at the time he came to me and told me that the lumber-yard was pressing him for money. I discovered that he had gone ahead and built the house, expecting that the stand would earn enough not only to enable him to buy the lot but to pay for the materials he used in building. To straighten out the tangle into which his over-optimism had led him, I arranged a mortgage for him with the building and loan association from the proceeds of which he paid for his lot, paid for the building materials for which he was already indebt, and then purchased enough materials with which to finish his home. His road stand folded up and disappeared the next winter--it never did make very much money. But in spite of this disappointment, he managed to earn enough during the periods when he worked to meet his loan payments, to keep adding to his homestead, until he finally had a substantial house, a garden and chicken-yard, and found himself living at a level of comfort and security which he had never before enjoyed.

Now if a family with virtually no capital and having to rely mainly on the earnings of occasional periods of work as a chauffeur, can establish itself in a country home, it ought to be possible for families with some capital and more earning power to do so. What such a family needs--in addition to courage--according to our experience is enough capital for the down payment on the purchase price of a place and enough cash to pay for such materials and equipment as cannot be purchased on credit. For the rest, they must rely upon their incomes. But that a modest income, especially during the first few years, will enable them not only to pay for their place but to develop it into a substantial and comfortable home, is not difficult to demonstrate on the basis of our own experience.

Assume that we are dealing with the problem of a family having enough capital for the first payment on a suitable place, enough cash with which to equip itself at least as well as we were able to, and with an income of $2,500 a year--approximately the income with which we worked our first year. Such a family living in the city would spend its income about as follows:

Rent	$600
Food	800
Clothing, etc.	500
Other expenses	600
Savings	?
Total	$2,500

Assuming that production upon the homestead increases gradually, and does not go as far toward self-sufficiency as is planned for the Dayton experiment, the family budget after moving to the country would look something like this:

Taxes and upkeep (in lieu of rent)	$100
Food	400
Clothing, etc.	300
Other expenses	450
Available for investment in the homestead	1,250
Total	$2,500

With the family producing its own shelter, instead of renting it, there is a saving of $500 a year between what would be spent for taxes and upkeep on their own home and that paid out in rent in the city. In the case of food, a cut of 50 per cent is possible the moment the garden, the orchard, and the chicken-yard contribute to the family larder. Between the sewing-room, the workshop, and the laundry, substantial savings are possible on clothing and other expenses. A fund of about $1,250 is therefore made available for investment in the homestead and its equipment, provided the family does all of its own work. To whatever extent servants are employed, this fund is reduced. In our own case, we much preferred to spend a part of it for help and to make our investment at a slower rate than to try to put so much into "saving" and take so much out of ourselves.

Surely I have said enough about the problems involved to make it clear why it is so difficult to answer the questions which are asked us about how much capital is needed for establishing a homestead in the country. Whenever I am asked the question I always think of that old poser, Which is the most important leg of a three-legged stool? The amount of capital needed is just one part of an equation in three terms, of which the other two are the income upon which the family can rely, and the degree to which the family is willing to endure pioneering.

[1] Since this study was made, the Bureau of Home Economics of the United States Department of Agriculture has made the following dietetic study. The "adequate diet' of the table might be called a "city" diet; the "very liberal diet suggested," a diet for homesteaders.

SUGGESTED FOOD BUDGETS FOR FARM FAMILIES

YEARLY SUPPLY FOR A FAMILY OF FIVE

	Unit	Adequate diet recommended when most of food is purchased	Very liberal diet suggested when there are good resources for family food production
Flour, cereals...............	lbs.	1130	400
Milk........................	gal.	360	400
Potatoes, sweet potatoes.......	bu.	14	10
Dried beans................	pk.	5	1
Tomatoes (citrus fruit)........	bu.	5	10
Leafy, green, yellow vegetables	lb.	320	585
Dried fruits..................	lb.	85	75
Other vegetables and fruit.....	lb.	365	1400
Butter, other fats............	lb.	200	165
Sugar.......................	lb.	180	200
Lean meat, poultry...........	lb.	250	620
Eggs........................	doz.	80	145

Chapter Nine - Security Versus Insecurity

MORE than a decade has passed since the Borsodi family took flight from the city. Experimentation, and interpretation of the experiments, on the Borsodi homestead finally reached a point where what had been learned had to be given utterance. The result was that protesting essay which I called *This Ugly Civilization.* It was an effort to interpret our quest of comfort and to develop from it a program which might lead to the conquest of comfort for individuals and families, if not for society as a whole. But it appeared in 1929, when the country was most deliriously celebrating the great boom of which Henry Ford was the prophet and mass production the gospel. Virtually no one wanted to be told that the whole industrialized world was mistaken; that there was another way and a better way of making a living and of providing ourselves with our hearts' desires than through organized, integrated, centralized labor. The way which I urged as desirable for the individual and essential to the salvation of society seemed romantic to some who read my book; practicable only for exceptional families to other readers, and hostile to the social centralization for which others were working.

The situation is different today.

As I write these lines, the newspapers are carrying a story to the effect that 15,252,000 men and women are unemployed. This means, according to *The Business Week*, which was responsible for this estimate, that during November, 1932, over 31.2 per cent of those who are normally employed in the United States were unable to earn a living: 46 per cent of those ordinarily employed in manufacturing; 45 per cent of those in mining; 40 per cent of those in forestry and fishing; 38 per cent of those in transportation; 35 per cent of those in domestic and personal service; 21 per cent of those in trade; I7per cent of those in agriculture; 10 per cent of those in public service; and 10per cent of our professional classes were unemployed. On the basis of one and a half dependents for each worker, 37,500,000 men, women, and children were directly affected by unemployment. And the situation since that estimate was made has become steadily worse. But these millions by no means number fully all those affected by the economic catastrophe which struck the country four years ago. It would be safe to say that again as many have had their standards of living sharply reduced by reductions in wages, by part-time work, and by declines in the price of what they produce or possess. And if we were to add those who live in terror of unemployment or of financial ruin, almost every person in the country would have to be included.

After nearly two centuries of industrial expansion and a full century of social reforms during which we destroyed monarchical tyranny, abolished human slavery, established a sound currency, reduced greatly the hours of labor, granted universal suffrage, and adopted countless other reforms, we find most of the country unemployed, reduced to poverty, dependent upon charity, in terror of ruin! In spite of the fact that the whole history of industrial expansion and social reform is filled with demonstrations of the impossibility of establishing security, much less happiness, by any measures which still leave the individual dependent for his living upon the industrial behemoth, what has thus far been done and what is now proposed by industrial leaders, politicians, and economists is in the main merely a continuance of the futile process of trying to produce prosperity by creating new industries, expanding credit, cheapening money, spreading work, shortening hours of labor, or establishing unemployment insurance.

Yesterday a young married man I know lost his position. The manufacturing company for which he had been working for four years as a salesman had to let him go. There had been nothing wrong with his work; the volume of the company's business had simply declined to a point which made it imperative that they lay off another man, and as the youngest salesman on the staff, he was the one to be dropped.

For months he and his wife had lived in terror of this possibility. A six-months-old baby, with the added financial responsibilities involved, had increased the fear with which they had contemplated the possibility of unemployment--at a time when millions were unemployed. Now the blow had fallen. With only three weeks' pay in his pocket, he and his wife, neither of them over twenty-five years of age, were simply terror-stricken. The landlord, the milkman, the butcher, the grocer--those upon whom they were immediately dependent for food and shelter—were suddenly transformed into menaces. Some idea of what this terror meant to this couple, as in one degree or another it has meant to millions of others in these troublous times, can be gathered from the fact that when my wife called the young mother on the phone, shortly after the husband left for work the morning following his discharge, to ask her not to remain alone if she was worrying, the hysterical answer received was that she couldn't come over just then--that she had suffered some kind of hysterical spell after her husband left her, had become nauseated, and vomited, but that after she straightened herself out, she would come right over.

Then there is the Segerstrom family. This is not their name--but it suggests their real name. Segerstrom is a carpenter. He has recently worked for me a little at odd jobs, so that I know him to be a hardworking, conscientious workman. He has an equally hard-working wife, and five children. Up to the collapse of the building boom in the fall of 1929, as far as I can now learn, he worked steadily month after month, earned high wages, and lived according to the conventional standard of skilled workingmen of his class. The Segerstroms then lived in a home which they had bought for a little down and a little each month; they owned a Ford car; they had the usual kind of furniture in their home, a radio, and all the comforts to which they felt an American standard of living entitled them. They had even managed to save a little money, some of which had been invested in securities recommended to them by the bank in which they deposited their money.

Then came the crash. Regular employment ended. At the end of the fourth winter of occasional work at odd jobs they had lost their home, lost and sold virtually all their furniture, and when we first heard of them they were living in a rented house in the country without a single modern convenience, and dependent upon the wood which they could cut in the woods about their house for fuel with which to keep warm during the wintry weather in this climate. His wife was working as a maid three days a week, and this managed to bring in just enough cash with which to pay the rent and occasionally buy some groceries. For the rest, they were engaged in a desperate struggle to act enough odd jobs and occasionally a little work at his trade of carpenter to keep the family from descending to the charitable agencies for relief.

As I write, Mrs. Segerstrom has lost her job as a maid, the family which had employed her having decided to move to another part of suburban New York. As far as I can judge, through no fault of their own but merely because of their blind reliance and dependence upon the scheme of living which is conventional in our industrial civilization, this family is going to become an object of public charity. In that respect their problem is the problem of millions of equally sober, decent, and useful human beings today.

Or take the case of the Smythes, which also is not their name, but suggests the two of them.

The Smythes were a rather proud couple in their fifties. They had no children. They had a nice home of their own in one of the most fashionable sections of northern Jersey. They drove a Chrysler, purchased when that meant more than it does today. Their home was much more than comfortably furnished. Smythe had been cashier and confidential man in some kind of brokerage business for over twenty years. His firm decided to liquidate, owing to the losses sustained when commodity prices slumped early in the depression. Through no fault of his own, Smythe found himself at fifty trying to secure any sort of position at all in which his knowledge of bookkeeping might be used. But not only was there an oversupply of bookkeepers--there was no demand at all for bookkeepers of his age. In spite of his efforts to locate himself for a period of nearly two years, the time finally came when the Smythes were reduced to a state in which they were without coal with which to heat their house, their telephone was being disconnected, and they had virtually nothing left to set upon the table. But so far as the neighbors could see, nothing was wrong. The Smythes seemed to be living substantially as they had been living for the past two years.

But one day the neighbors became conscious of the fact that the Smythes had disappeared. Investigation showed that two days before Smythe had picked up a hatchet, split open his wife's skull as she lay in bed, gone down to his garage, started the motor in his car, lain down by the exhaust, and asphyxiated himself.

Then there was the case of Jones—which promises to end more hopefully than that of Smythe.

One day I received a letter from a man named Jones, or a name very similar to Jones, begging the privilege of an interview. He had read *This Ugly Civilization,* he wrote, and had a straightforward question he wanted to put to me. He asked me to give him a few minutes in which to put his case before me if I possibly could spare the time, since he was prepared to stake all he had upon my answer to it. Of course I saw him. And this is the story he told me.

"Mr. Borsodi," he said, "I am an accountant. The firm for which I used to work failed just about a year ago. I had worked for them for nine years. But I had made such a good record and had managed to save $1,500, so that I wasn't particularly worried. But that was a year ago. Since that time I have walked the streets of New York without a single, real chance to secure any kind of a position which would enable me to support my wife and daughter. I have tried almost everything. I have answered every help-wanted advertisement in the newspapers, registered with all sorts of employment agencies, called on all my friends and relatives and almost everybody with whom I was even remotely acquainted, in an effort to find some sort of work which I might do. Fortunately, my wife was able to secure occasional employment in a department store, clerking at the counter. She would leave our little girl with her grandmother during the period she worked. But in spite of the money she managed to earn, and a little which I managed to pickup, we have been steadily wiping out our savings. Even after practicing every sort of economy, the rent makes big holes in our savings each month, though we have managed to even reduce this by doubling up with my wife's parents. Today I have only $500 left of my original savings. And I can see the end of that this coming year.

"Like lots of other men, when tired of walking around, I have dropped into the public libraries to read and get my mind off my troubles. About a week ago I happened to pick up your book, *This Ugly Civilization,* and I raced through it--it seemed to be written just for me. I don't need to tell you how it affected me. It seemed to furnish the complete answer to just such problems as the one with which I had been struggling. But what a ghastly joke that I should have stumbled upon your book only after most of my capital had been sunk in the sheer cost of keeping my family alive this past year. I have been torturing myself ever since thinking about what I might have done to maintain them if I had worked in a garden of my own instead of just tramping the streets of New York trying to find jobs under conditions such as prevail at present!

"Now, Mr. Borsodi, the question I would like to ask you is this: Should I take a chance with my last $500 and try to get to the country, where we would have a chance at least to partially support ourselves, even if we couldn't do it completely right away, or should I take a chance on finding work before my $500 has all gone to the milkman, the grocer, and the landlord? Is it possible, with only $500 cash, to make a start toward the independence of a job which you advocate in your book? This is the question which my wife and I have been debating night after night ever since I read your book. What do you think? I am perfectly willing to work. I think I can make a success of such a homestead as you describe; my wife is willing to work just as hard as I am--but will $500 enable us to make a start toward independence?"

The terror, the suffering, and the tragedies of my young neighbor, of the Segerstrom family, of the Smythes, of Jones the accountant, and of most of the millions of men and women who are unemployed today, are consequences of that mysterious phenomenon known as the business cycle—mysterious as to cause but not as to effects--which periodically produces in our industrial civilization a decline in the volume of trade, a sharp drop in prices, a shrinkage in the amount of credit, a decrease in the demand for goods, a decline in the volume of production, and in consequence an increase in the number of unemployed. Men and women at work in factories and offices and stores, workers in building and in railroading, all the myriads engaged in the services, trades, and professions--barbers, waiters, actors, artists, reporters, architects, who are busily at work during periods of prosperity and good times--suddenly find themselves out of work, while those who remained employed find themselves in most cases working only a part of each week and at lower wages and salaries. A force beyond their control and in most cases utterly beyond their comprehension suddenly leaves them without the income with which to pay rent, buy food, purchase clothing, and pay their debts.

But equally through no fault of their own, other millions of cogs in our industrialized world and interdependent economic system find themselves periodically without the income which will enable them to buy the necessaries of life because of seasonal unemployment, or technological unemployment, or what I call style unemployment. Just as the winter season tends to throw building-workers out of employment, and the invention of new machines and new techniques tends to throw out of employment those engaged in manufacturing staple and established products, so style changes with their shifts in demand from wool dress goods to silk, from short skirts to long skirts, from crockery to glassware, and from phonographs to radios, create unemployment for workers in some industries even though employment is created for other workers in other industries.

And quite without regard to whether the cause is seasonal, or cyclical, or technological, or style unemployment, all these victims of unemployment are alike in this respect, that they are periodically unable to support themselves and their families through no fault of their own because of *their dependence upon what they earn as a cog in some part of the complex machinery of our factory-dominated civilization.* If the period of unemployment proves to be a short one, their savings are reduced or wiped out and debts accumulated which impair their ability to save for some time after they are again employed, while if the period proves a long one--as long as the period through which twelve or thirteen millions of Americans are now struggling--they are apt to become social charges, to become utterly demoralized by public charity, and in the end not only to loathe but to become revolters against a social system which subjects them to such treatment.

The popular formula of social reformers for mitigating the evils of unemployment is unemployment insurance--which deals with the effect of the trouble, and the popular formula for ending unemployment altogether—is to have the government in some way or other control if not own and operate all industry.

Neither the formula for mitigation—which merely shifts the cost of unemployment from those unemployed to those employed, nor the formula for ending unemployment--which merely shifts the control of our economic life from capitalists to public officials of some sort or other--appeals particularly to me. Neither furnishes, in my opinion, a cure for the fundamental defect in our present economic system--the excessive dependence of individual men and women for their livelihoods upon the smooth functioning of nation-wide and even international economic activities.

There remains to be considered the formula of despair--that the unemployed should leave our cities and turn to farming to support their families. But the modern farmer, specializing in the production for sale of wheat or cotton or milk, has just as difficult a problem in employing himself profitably as has the wageworker or the office-worker. For the unemployed to ex-change their present dependence upon industrial activity for dependence upon agricultural prices--for them to exchange the insecurities of the labor market for the insecurities of the grain or cattle or produce markets--is merely to jump out of the frying pan into the fire.

The only reason that everybody does not as yet recognize the fact that the average farmer has a problem of employment is because the evil effects of a decline in the price of the crop he produces do not put him on charity as quickly as the evil effects of a decline in the sales of the products of some in-dustry. With declines in sales of manufactured products, industrial workers are promptly laid off or fired, but with declines in agricultural prices, unem-ployment only appears after foreclosure of farms for non-payment of interest and taxes leaves farmers without farms on which to work. It is true, of course, that the evil effects of dependence upon the general condition of business are smaller in degree in the case of farmers, even for those who specialize in cash crops such as wheat and cotton and hogs, because most farmers tend to produce some of their own necessities of life. If they own their own farms, they at least provide their own shelter instead of renting it. If they have a vegetable-garden and orchard, or a cow and some chickens, they at least produce some of their own foodstuffs. Even though they are in the long run affected disastrously by their dependence upon the growing of crops sold in the produce markets at prices fixed by the total supply and de-mand for what they produce, this limited degree of production for use gives to farmers in general a position somewhat more secure than that of industri-al workers. But that is all. The more dependent the farmer is upon his cash crop, the more he is apt to suffer from the problem of employment.

The essence of the matter is that when the farmer shifted his productive activities from production for his own use to production for sale, he subject-ed himself to economic insecurities of a type roughly comparable in nature to the insecurities to which the wage-worker and the office-worker are now subjected. The farmer at one time was self-sufficient. He not only produced his own foodstuffs; he produced his own fabrics and clothing. Weaving and knitting were as much the activities of the homestead as farming. Sheep fur-nished him wool; the cattle he slaughtered furnished him leather; a wood lot furnished him fuel for heat and cooking. The farmer of the past, in most in-stances, spent the part of the year when farming operations could not be per-formed because of the season, operating grist-mills or lumber-mills, or work-ing at some craft or trade. Such a life had only the insecurities which nature itself seems to impose upon human activities, and the possible damage from storm and drought, from locusts and hail, was reduced by storage of supplies and diversification of production. The threat of dispossession and unem-ployment which the dependence of the farmer upon the cash market has brought into farming was then unknown. Today farmers have abandoned not only the production of fabrics and clothing, but on about 20 per cent of the farms in this country there is not even a cow or a chicken; on 30 per cent there is not a single hog, and on approximately 90 percent not even one sheep. What is more, on many of the farms in our banner agricultural states no gardens are kept and almost every article of food is purchased at the store. If the unemployed of the cities turn to that kind of farming, they will merely have exchanged one kind of economic insecurity for another.

What is called subsistence farming, however, is a step, though only a step, in the right direction.

But no return to farming, no establishment of unemployment insurance, and not even the planning or socialization of industrial activities, will furnish an adequate alternative way of life to the artist and craftsman for whom the problem of living includes some sort of escape from the repetitive work which is all that an industrial civilization offers them.

A short time ago I received the following letter from a man with quite a reputation as a poet. The situation with which he has been confronted by our industrial civilization is quite typical of that with which countless numbers of talented men and women are today faced. Since my book appeared I have received scores of similar letters:

The question that persisted in my mind after reading the necessarily incomplete account of your ideas and their operation in that interview, is this: Can your plans obviously sound and salutary in their application to a crisis like the present, be made continuously operative; not only, that is, to provide self-sustaining work instead of wasteful charity to the jobless victims of hard times, but to afford a continuous way of living through all kinds of times? But by "way of living" I do not mean an existence just beyond the margin of want, nor a way devoid of participation in the characteristic conveniences of modern times; I do not mean a mere throw-back to the simplicity that characterized American farm and rural-town life up to fifty or sixty years ago; but I mean, can a community organized on your principles not only afford a sane, healthful existence to its members, but also, as long as a capitalistic organization of society endures, a modest and constant increment of usable wealth in the form of money, to give access to the world and its goods outside the community, to provide insurance against age and casualty, and to provide some inheritance for the next generation?

Consider my own position. Born and raised in a city, reared and educated not to use my hands but to use my head to "get along" in life; overlooked by nature, however, in the distribution of the acquisitive instinct; I have drifted and tumbled along through life, never producing anything (except some negligible literature and criticism), but precariously holding and losing various parasitical jobs, seldom quite earning my way. Finally comes a small inheritance, some of which was lost in Wall Street; the bulk of it, small enough, is in the soundest investments the country affords; which nowadays yield diminished income, have in part lost their liquidity, and are slowly melting as I draw on them to eke out earnings, by myself and my wife, insufficient to meet the expenses of a modest scale of living. I can in the nature of things have no program but to live carefully and keep alert for another chance at parasitical employment, in government or in private business.

Is there a saner way, not as a temporary expedient, but as a permanent program? --and a way which would enable us not only to keep housed, clothed, and fed, but to have some freedom of movement, some chance to participate in the good things which our urbanized, industrialized, capitalistic civilization does afford, along with its evils?

That there is such a program is shown by the letters which follow, one from a letter received shortly after *This Ugly Civilization* was published and the other, from a letter received from the same writer two and a half years later:

I have just finished reading *This Ugly Civilization,* and cannot rest until I have made an effort to let you know what it means to me. Though I attained the age of thirty only a few days ago, I have long been preaching many of the reforms you advocate. And as librarian and instructor in an institution filled with herd-minded students and instructors, controlled by quantity-minded capitalists and politicians, and located in a hopelessly conventional and very religious college community, you may be able to imagine the inhibitions and morbid mental confinement of my existence. Having the sweet companionship of your book in such an iron-clad environment of bondage is comparable to the Mormon conception of Joseph Smith finding the golden tablets.

As librarian I am ever searching the publications which list and advertise new books and when I first saw yours advertised, I began to hope that my long search, with its many disappointments, had at last found its reward. In reading page after page I rejoiced to find not only my own ideas, but a great many more which I had not yet arrived at, all expressed in clear, logical language. You see, for years I have been slowly yet carefully gathering notes...building up my case against the masses who control my every action...gradually preparing myself for the time when I might stand high on my firm and ever-accumulating foundation of fact and reason and denounce them all. Somehow I can't get over the feeling that the book was prepared especially for me, that I might grasp it eagerly: a complete and carefully constructed basis upon which to rest my own peculiar philosophy of life.

My most cherished dream has long been the establishment of my own "little island of intelligence and beauty" that should stand gallantly and undefiled "amidst the chaotic seas of human stupidity and ugliness." Nearly a year ago I selected and purchased ten acres of land and will soon be able to make the final payment on it. We managed to erect a habitable building, dig and equip a well, and raise a small flock of pullets; and my dear old mother is heroically holding the fort until we can achieve the financial status necessary for me to join her. And if nothing happens this should be within the present year. Then, with my mother, the two children of my deceased brother, and a distant young lady who has promised to share the transvaluation with me, I plan to sacrifice the present emoluments and future prospects of my profession and begin the great experiment of my life.

Your book comes at an opportune time to serve as my handbook of procedure and inspiration. And, having the encouragement it has brought and my plans for the reasonable life so far along, I feel sufficiently independent to begin to voice more openly the ideas which I have so long considered in secret. Hereafter I shall not only speak on the subject, but I intend to quote appropriate passages from your book. Of course I shall place one or more copies of it on the library shelves. However, there is every reason to believe that, if it reaches the hands of any of the more conservative members of the faculty (and it probably will), they will request its removal because of the remarks on religion.

But why worry over trifles?

About two and a half years later and over a year after the writer of this letter had moved to his own "island of intelligence and beauty," I received the following letter from him:

Since receiving your letter some two years ago, I have had ample time to consider the truth of your statement that the cards were stacked against the farmer. However, we may console ourselves with the fact that the farmer is not now suffering alone. Here I did not plan to farm on a large scale, but only to have some chickens. With the chickens I have used plenty of caution and as yet have not suffered any losses. Despite the depression, things have gone on quite well. I have a position at the local university library and divide my time between this seat of learning and the ranch. We have a comfortable home, ten acres and the first three units of the chicken arrangement finished and it is all paid for so we feel fairly independent.

We are all well satisfied and like the open spaces more all the time. In some respects our situation is ideal. Although it takes less than fifteen minutes to reach the city, we are far enough out to hear the coyotes howl now and then. We enjoy (more than I had thought possible) the attractions of the city along with the peace and freedom of the desert. I think this type of community will be more and more popular in the future. As yet no house is closer than a quarter of a mile to us, yet we have all the essential conveniences of the city such as electricity for light, power, and heating; telephone, daily newspaper service, all kinds of city delivery such as ice, coal, milk, laundry, and the like.

But what I like most is the diversified work that I have to do out here, it is such a delightful variety in contrast to the routine work I have been used to. Out here no day seems half long enough, for there is everything from writing poetry to cleaning the hen- house to be done, and every type of activity is interesting.

Need anything more be said on this subject?

For this man, and for any man who will similarly start on the road to independence, the problem of employment can hardly be said to exist.

Chapter Ten - Independence Versus Dependence

IT IS a simple dictate of the heart which says: If a man is hungry, feed him; if he is naked, clothe him; if he is homeless, shelter him.

But it is a dictate neither of the heart nor of the head, which says, if a man is unemployed, support him.

Yet in one way or another, most of what is being done to relieve the distress and suffering of the millions who are unemployed as a result of the depression amounts to nothing more than that those who are employed shall support those who are not. Most relief, and most plans for relief, are merely measures for supporting (or tiding over) the unemployed for that indefinite period of time which they will have to spend looking for work or waiting for work to turn up. That home relief, and food tickets, and bread lines, are measures for supporting the unemployed is obvious. It is not so obvious--but it is nevertheless the same thing--to "make work" for them; that is, to invent such work as cleaning the parks of a city as a mere excuse for doling out cash to them. And itis still the same thing--supporting the unemployed--to make those who are employed "share" their work with them so that both shall be partly employed and partly unemployed. And many of the remedies for unemployment, such as unemployment insurance, however ingeniously they may be dressed up, are still merely measures for supporting the unemployed. For unemployment insurance is merely a device by which contributions from those employed, from the employers, and from the government are doled out to support those who are unemployed.

My first point, therefore, is this: I am utterly opposed to all measures for relief which upon analysis show themselves to be mere measures for supporting the unemployed. I am opposed to them on three grounds.

First, because they are evasions of the problem of the unemployed. They are not solutions of their problem. The public gives for relief, and the public pays taxes for relief, and the public hopes, just like Mr. Micawber, that "something will turn up" to end the depression and that the problem will then vanish.

Secondly, I am opposed to mere support of the unemployed because of the financial drain which such support inflicts upon their friends and relatives (to whom they first turn); to the financial drain which it puts upon industry to whatever extent industry and commerce try to support them; and to the drain upon taxpayers to whatever extent municipal, and state, and national funds are used to support them.

Finally, I am opposed to them because they are demoralizing to the unemployed. They break down their self-respect. They destroy their sense of responsibility and self-reliance; in short, they pauperize them.

There is, however, in my opposition to supporting the unemployed, and what I said in the beginning about the imperious duty of feeding the hungry, clothing the naked, and sheltering the homeless, no contradiction. What we do for the temporary assistance of unfortunate fellow creatures, particularly when their misfortune is not of their own contriving, is true charity. I do not like the word charity, though it is the only one that I can think of in this connection. For this sort of assistance is really a species of hospitality; when we give this sort of temporary assistance we are only doing, indirectly, what used to be the universal custom for us to do for every stranger who knocked at the doors of the pioneer homesteads of America's past.

But if we are not to support the unemployed—beyond giving them what I have spoken of as temporary assistance--what then are we to do for them at this time?

I have an answer for this question. And unlike most of the answers to it, it is so completely the obvious answer that I dare not state it until some sort of background for it has been prepared. For my answer cannot be fully appreciated, it cannot be fully understood, its complete practicality cannot be realized, until we have first thought through completely what the problem of unemployment really is.

We have in this country at present about fifteen million men and women, formerly employed, who are today unemployed. In the aggregate, this army of ex-factory-workers, ex-farm-laborers, ex-railroad-workers, ex-office and store workers, has created such a stupendous and complex problem that it is easy for us to forget that in its fundamentals the problem of every one of these fifteen million human beings is exactly the same. If we consider it from the standpoint of the individual unemployed workers, we shall avoid the danger of being deceived by the sheer size of the problem. Now if we consider it this way, here is what we find: John Doe, who was formerly employed-- perhaps in an office, perhaps in a factory--is now no longer employed by that office or that factory. What is more, he cannot find employment in other offices or factories.

What, now, is the difference in John Doe's situation before unemployment and after? Before unemployment and while he was still employed, he received every pay day a certain sum of money as wages or salary for the time he spent working for the firm which employed him. John Doe, if he was the breadwinner of a family, took this money and with it his family bought food and clothes and entertainment; they paid for housing in the form of rent (or if they owned their own home, in the form of taxes or interest), and they paid the installments on debts which they had contracted in buying their furniture, their automobile, their home, and if they were thrifty, they saved a part of the pay for a rainy day by depositing it in a savings-bank, paying for insurance, or in some cases actually investing it in stocks and bonds.

After unemployment, John Doe no longer received any wages or salary. If the family had been fortunate and thrifty up to that time and had accumulated something in the way of savings, these savings were drawn upon to meet current expenses. When the savings were exhausted, they began to sell their investments, their automobile, their home, their furniture, in order to get the money with which to maintain the family. Then they began to borrow from friends and relatives in order to do so; they bought on credit from the merchants whom they had formerly been able to pay regularly; finally, when all these means of securing the things they needed to keep body and soul together were exhausted, they turned to the charitable and relief agencies. Then these agencies began to give them the money directly with which to buy them or they gave them indirectly--by paying it to those stores upon whom John Doe and his family were given orders for food or by paying it to the landlords who furnished the shelter for the family.

In the meantime, what had John Doe been doing? He was doing what he was expected to do--spending his time looking for employment; going from one factory to another, from one employment agency to the next, answering one help-wanted advertisement after another, and trying to find odd jobs for which he could gee some money to help in the emergency.

And when physically or spiritually too exhausted to spend his time looking for work, he spent it waiting for business to pick up, so that he could get back to his old job, whatever it may have been. And in doing this, and spending his time in this way, he is encouraged by virtually all the relief agencies established to cope with the depression up to the present time.

But not only the relief agencies. He is encouraged in the course outlined by the whole commercial world. All our big industrial and financial leaders tell him that he has only to wait--that in time a readjustment will be effected and that then employment will again become normal. And they tell him to remember that while he is unemployed their capital is unemployed. While he has to worry about himself and his family, they have the burden not only of trying to manage their plants and to employ as many people as possible, but also the worry of protecting the investors in their business. So he is assured that everybody is in the same boat; that it is only necessary to avoid rocking the boat and sooner or later the pilots will get it back safely into harbor.

And of course the "pilots" or political leaders tell him substantially the same thing. Great economic forces about which they are often extremely vague have upset the markets of the world. For the moment, they are just as powerless in coping with these economic forces as they used to be powerless in the face of natural forces such as famines and plagues. While the government and Congress experiments with one expedient after another in its efforts to create a revival of trade, a feeling of confidence among business men, and a rise in prices, there is nothing for John Doe and the millions like him to do but wait until things pick up again.

But what is even worse, our social reformers in slightly different words tell him virtually the same thing. There is nothing particularly wrong, according to them, with the complex industrial system which had formerly employed him. It is still a marvelous system, far superior to any which had ever previously been relied upon by mankind for supplying it with its needs and desires. *What is wrong is the control or ownership of the system.* It is the profit system, not the industrial system, which is responsible for his plight. According to them, all that is necessary is to establish a plan board—to adopt a five-year plan of our own--or to have the state take over the ownership of industry altogether and run it for use and not for profit. In the meantime, while we are still struggling with the follies of capitalism and individualism, all that can be done as a sort of stop-gap for the emergency is to establish government employment agencies, increase the numbers employed directly or indirectly by the government, and adopt a system of unemployment insurance.

I disagree with all of them. The unemployed, if they can't be given work here and now by our industrial system, should not be asked to live half hungry, half naked, half cold, while waiting for business to pick up. Above all they should not be fed upon promises of blissful security in the distant future--after our reformers have finished tinkering with the industrial system and remolding all our institutions nearest to their heart's desire.

When a family cannot support itself, and secure the food, clothing, and shelter it needs by getting employment in a factory, or an office, or a store, the only sensible thing for it to do is to support itself by producing these things for itself on its own homestead. If the unemployed are to be made secure at least as to the needs of life, nothing short of this is adequate. They surely cannot be made secure by shifting their dependence for their livelihood from the business cycle to the political cycle, neither of which is capable of coping with the inherent insecurity of industrial production.

Let us not fool ourselves about what the future holds in store for us. There are at present no grounds whatever for expecting any return to normal business very soon. No responsible student of business conditions expects any complete solution of the problem of unemployment during the coming year. Eventually another period of expansion may come, but as in the depression of 1873, it may take ten years to get back to full employment again.

These facts are so generally recognized that everywhere plans are being made for the continuation of direct relief programs. In New York City, where the situation is in many ways typical of that in all our industrial cities, there are over 200,000 unemployed families. Without including the uncounted number of destitute single men and women, this means that over 1,000,000human beings are now dependent upon relief and charity for their food, clothing, and shelter. With no prospects of business improvement, plans are being made to support this number of families for the whole of 1933. It is true that from time to time some of these families secure work and so become self-supporting, but others are laid off to take their place. The same issue of the New York which carried a story about a slight improvement in business in the fall of 1932, carried another story about the laying off of 2,800 men by a single corporation in New York City.

At the request of the Emergency Home Relief Bureau, the New York City Welfare Agencies prepared a budget covering the merest necessities for these families. On the basis of that budget, the taxpayers, the contributors to relief funds, and the relatives of the unemployed, are faced with the appalling problem of raising $161,370,000 for the support of these families for the single year of 1933.

Now what does this sort of relief mean to the individual family?

While the breadwinners of the family are supposed to be out looking for work, each family of five is to receive a bare subsistence ration of $6.85 in food each week; a minimum clothing budget of $2.45 per week; a fuel and light budget of $2.95 per week; a minimum rent budget of $4.50 per week. This is a total for each family, each week of $15.85, without provision for accident and illness, birth and death. In the course of one year, even on this minimum basis, $824.20 will have to be expended on each unemployed family consisting of five persons.

Eight hundred dollars, at the present purchasing power of the dollar, is a lot of money. Yet I know, upon the basis of my own experience, that it is more than is required as the initial capital with which to establish a self-sufficient homestead.

It is much more than the amount with which many of our pioneer forefathers established themselves in the country and supported themselves indefinitely.

If even half that sum--not more than five hundred dollars--were to be intelligently laid out for land and lumber, for seeds, livestock, and implements, the average family could produce for itself the bare essentials of living, and have plenty of time left for part-time or seasonal employment in industry. With proper instruction and leadership, not much more than half the sum which is now being spent to support a family for a year would be sufficient to take one family permanently off the relief list. It would do more. It would not only enable them to support themselves; it would ultimately make it possible for them to repay the money and materials furnished them.

The problem of unemployment would for them have been solved. The drain upon the community for their support would have been ended, the self-respect of the unemployed restored.

We have raised hundreds of millions already for unemployment relief. Since we have used it merely to support the unemployed, we now find ourselves face to face with the necessity of doing the same thing over and over again. Instead of spending more and more millions to support the unemployed while the depression is dragging its weary way over the years, why shouldn't we use the public's "will-to-give" to enable the unemployed to support themselves? Why shouldn't we furnish them land, tools, lumber, seed, livestock, wool, leather, raw materials of all kinds to enable them to establish themselves once again in the homesteads which they should never have abandoned as many of them did perhaps generations back? Above all, while doing so, let us use our universities and our social agencies for the purpose of guiding and instructing those of them who may have forgotten, or never learned, how to wrest the necessities of life directly from their own land and their own efforts.

We should not only relieve them temporarily.

If we did it on a sufficiently large scale, we would end the problem of un-employment for the whole country, and end it permanently.

For a hundred years America has been developing its factory system.

Year after year we have been building up our cities; steadily we have been shifting our population from the country (where they used to at one time support themselves) into cities (where they became wholly dependent upon industry for their livelihood). And while doing this, we have boasted about the glorious conquests of the machine age. The machine age was shortening the hours of labor; it was annihilating space and enabling us to fly; it was furnishing even the humblest of us magical amusements--"pictures" which moved and talked, and "radios" which brought song and speech on the waves of the air.

Yet today, millions of the beneficiaries of this machine age are no longer worrying about maintaining the high standard of living about which we have been boasting. They have lost their aspirations for two-car garages, and new models each year. They are no longer trying to keep up with the Joneses.

We have dotted the landscape with our factories. We have filled the cities with skyscrapers. We have covered the continent with a network of rails and roadways, But in spite of all these things, we have been unable to furnish the American people security even as to such bare essentials as food and cloth-ing and shelter.

During the depression of 1837 they were told that the Central Bank of the United States was responsible for the country's depression. So they abol-ished it.

During the depression of 1854 they were told that the state banks and their wildcat currency were responsible for the country's depression. So they established national banks and a national currency.

During the depression of 1907, they were told that the lack of a central banking system was responsible for the country's depressions. So they estab-lished the Federal Reserve system.

Today they are being told that the lack of balance between production and consumption is responsible for the country's depression, and that economic planning will end the country's depressions.

During the last few years they have read endlessly in books and magazines and newspapers about the wonders of the Russian five-year plan. They have been told that planning was not only the way out of the depression, but also the way to security and a better way of life.

Once again they are pricking up their hopes. Once again they are asking themselves whether at last the doctors haven't found the one thing which will tame the machine age and furnish the country the security it has long been denied. But suppose they establish a plan board for industry. Suppose America adopts a five-year plan of her own. Suppose it tries out economic planning. It has tried nearly everything else. I have no doubt that it will try planning, too.

And then it shall be once again disappointed.

After all, the planning board will have to be composed of human beings, and human beings are all too human. They make mistakes. Even if the members of the Supreme Economic Council, or whatever the planning board would be called, prove all to be chaste, incorruptible, and without ambition (which I refuse to believe a reasonable expectation), there is no guarantee that even the most virtuous board will not make mistakes.

The Russians, in spite of their revolutionary zeal, have made them. Their five-year plan called for the socialization of agriculture. Farming was to be mechanized. Farming was to be collectivized. The little, inefficient farms of the peasants were to be merged into giant, efficient farms run by machinery, and transformed into wheat factories.

Within a year and a half from the time they started to carry out their plan, the Russians socialized more of these farms than they expected to take over in five years. The plan was hailed as a tremendous success, not only by the Russians, but by the advocates of planning everywhere in the world. But, unfortunately, something went wrong. The planners miscalculated. With that sublime indifference to the human equation which they borrowed from engineering, the Gosplan overlooked how the peasants would react to this appropriation of what had been their personal property. During the process of converting the little farms into giant farms, millions of horses and cows and pigs and chickens were slaughtered by the peasants who couldn't see eye to eye with the agents of the Soviet. Within a short time, not only was there a shortage of meat for the table, there were no horses for plowing and cultivating and harvesting. The effect upon food production was cumulatively bad. Today, in spite of their five-year plan, in spite of their pathetic faith in the efficacy of socialism, the whole of Russia is on a starvation diet. True, some sections of the population--the proletariat--are specially favored. But then so are certain sections of the population with us, only we call them the rich. And as for the unfortunate fact that with us some of the unemployed are subjected to inhuman suffering--the Russians match that by subjecting the kulaks, the nobles, and the clergy to similar inhuman suffering.

The truth about the matter is that neither the things proposed in previous depressions nor the economic planning proposed in this one is capable of ending the insecurity from which we suffer.

Insecurity and industrialism are Siamese twins. You cannot have one without having to accept the other.

Insecurity is the price we pay for our dependence upon industrialism for the essentials of life.

A very old Biblical story makes it clear that when one man becomes dependent upon another for the opportunity to secure the food with which to keep himself alive, he may be forced to sacrifice his birthright of freedom and happiness. Isaac, it will be remembered, was a wealthy man. He had rich lands, large flocks, and many servants. Esau was his oldest son and favorite. Custom made him his father's exclusive heir. But he was a reckless hunter, while his more conservative brother Jacob, who coveted Esau's birthright, was a farmer. The story of what happened to Esau, as the Bible tells it, runs as follows:

And Jacob had pottage.

And Esau came from the hunt, and he was faint.

And Esau said to Jacob: "Feed me, I pray thee, with that same pottage for I am faint."

And Jacob said, "Sell me this day thy birthright."

And Esau said, "Behold I am at the point to die, and what profit shall this birthright do me?"

And Jacob said, "Swear me this day."

And Esau swore to him and sold his birthright unto Jacob.

Then Jacob gave Esau bread and pottage of lentils, and he did eat and drink and rose up, and went his way.

Thus Esau lost his birthright.

Surely it is unnecessary to draw amoral. Surely it is plain that no man can afford to be dependent upon some other man for the bare necessities of life without running the risk of losing all that is most precious to him. Yet that is precisely and exactly what most of us are doing today. Everybody seems to be dependent upon some one else for the opportunity to acquire the essentials of life. The factory-worker is dependent upon the man who employs him; both of them are dependent upon the salesmen and the retailers who sell the goods they make, and all of them are dependent upon the consuming public, which may not want, or may not be able, to buy what they may have made.

What the depression has done has been immensely to increase the evil effects of this interdependence. What difference does it make to the man who is unemployed why the demand for coal, or for automobiles, or for cotton goods has fallen off? All he knows is that for some reason beyond his control he has been laid off. If being laid off merely resulted in his having to curtail his enjoyment of the luxuries of life, the situation would be bad enough, but at least it would not be tragic. But when being laid off means that he and his wife and children may be deprived of food, when it means that they may find themselves without a roof over their heads, when it means that they may be ragged and cold and sick, except in so far as charity helps them--then you have stark, staring tragedy.

Compare the position of the millions of men who are today unemployed to the position of our pioneer forefathers of a hundred years ago. At the beginning of the last century, Brillat-Savarin, the famous Frenchman who wrote *The Physiology of Taste,* made a long visit to the United States. In the fourth chapter of his book he tells the story of a visit of several weeks which he made to a farm which is now within the densely populated region of Hartford, Connecticut. As he was leaving, his host took him aside and said:

"You behold in me, my dear sir, a happy man, if there is one on earth; everything you see around you, and what you have seen at my house, is produced on my farm. These stockings have been knitted by my daughters, my shoes and clothes came from my herds; they, with my garden and my farmyard, supply me with plain and substantial food. The greatest praise of our government is that in Connecticut there are thousands of farmers quite as content as myself, and whose doors, like mine, are never locked."

Today the farm on which that happy man once lived is cut up into city streets and covered with city buildings. The men and women of Hartford no longer produce their own food, clothing, and shelter. They work for them in stores and offices and factories. And in that same city, descendants of that pioneer farmer are probably walking the streets, not knowing what to do in order to be able to secure food, clothing and shelter.

Postlude

The New Frontier

SINCE I made the study of homesteading for Dayton, Ohio, described in Chapter Ten, last winter, the First Homestead Unit of Dayton has become a reality. A farm of 160 acres located about three miles from the city limits has been purchased and laid out in three-acre plots; the old farm buildings have been rehabilitated for use as a community center; thirty-five families are now developing the tract, building homes, and planting crops. It is possible, therefore, to add to this book a detailed account based upon an actual rather than a theoretical adventure in homesteading by a group of families developing the same idea upon which the individual adventure of the Borsodi family was predicated. The Dayton project is due mainly to the vision and leadership of Dr. Elizabeth H. Nutting, the Executive Secretary of the Character-Building Division of the Council of Social Agencies of Dayton. If I have hope for the success of this particular experiment, it is primarily due to the fact that Dr. Nutting's leadership is educational in philosophy.

But Dr. Nutting could not have developed the project but for the fortunate coincidence that Dayton possessed at the same time a group of social-minded men and women in key positions in the city's public life. Outstanding in this group are Mrs. Virginia P. Wood, Chairman of the Character-Building Division of the Council of Social Agencies; Mr. Arch Mandel, Executive Secretary of the Dayton Bureau of Community Service; Mr. E. V. Stoecklein, Director of Public Welfare of the city; Mr. S. H. Thai, of S. H. Thai, Inc., Chairman of the Homestead Committee; and Mr. Walter Locke, editor of *The Dayton News.* Other members of the Unit Committee of the Council of Social Agencies, as the group sponsoring the movement is called, are the Rev. Chas. Lyon Seasholes, President of the committee, Pastor of the First Baptist Church; Mr. Wm. A. Chryst, Consulting Engineer, Delco Products Company; Robert G. Corwin, attorney, McMahon, Corwin, Landis and Markham, President of the Council of Social Agencies; J. N. Garwood, Assembly Foreman, National Cash Register Company; Mrs. Daisy T. Greene; Mr. W. A. Keyes, Vice-President, Bureau of Community Service; Mrs. Mabel M. Pierce; Mr. Frank D. Slutz, educator; Mr. N. M. Stanley, President, The Univis Corporation; Mr. E. C. Wells, Vice-President, Platt Iron Works; Gen. Geo. H. Wood, Veteran's Administration, U. S. A. An advisory board in accounting, agriculture, arts and crafts, engineering, health, home economics, law, and education, including many nationally known personalities, is assisting the committee. Under the chairmanship of Dr. Harold Rugg of Columbia University, the national implications of the Dayton experiment are being studied by a group interested in education particularly from the standpoint of adult education. This committee includes Dr. C. F. Ansley of Columbia University, Dr. B. H. Bode of Ohio State University, Dr. Wm. H. Kilpatrick of Columbia University, Dr. E. C. Lindeman, New York School for Social Work, and Dr. H. A. Overstreet of the College of the City of New York. Dr. Nutting and I are also members of this group.

The self-sacrificing members of Dr. Nutting's staff in starting the movement should not be forgotten Howard Keeler, production manager; T. J. Wood, assistant production manager; Hazel Lehman, bookkeeper; Margaret Hutchison, Hazel Boe, Alberta Tucker, secretaries. Their willingness to work day and night and in most cases for no more than "board and room," has been one of the most important factors in the development of this experiment.

An account of the movement which I wrote at the request of Freda Kirchway, one of the editors of *The Nation,* and which appeared in that magazine on April 19, 1933, is reprinted here because it furnishes a compact summary of what took place up to that time.

Dayton Makes Social History

"Dayton, Ohio, is setting the stage for an important economic, social, and educational experiment. Out of the Production Units, established in the summer of last year, is growing a movement to ring the city of Dayton with what will be known as Homestead Units. The Homestead Unit represents an attempt to solve the dilemmas of the machine age along entirely new lines.

"In one respect the Dayton movement is quite different from the hundreds of self-help, barter, and scrip movements which have sprung up all over the country. It is an experiment in production for use as against production for sale or exchange. From the very beginning the leaders of the Dayton group have had in mind not only a temporary solution for the problem of the unemployed but a permanently better way of living for every man, woman, and child now struggling for happiness in our industrial civilization.

"The original Production Units, of which there are now ten, are located in various sections of the city. They now have a membership of around 800 families and are the principal source of support of nearly 4,000 men, women, and children. The tenth unit was organized the week I was in Dayton in the middle of January. A unit was also being organized in one of the largest high schools in the city to include boys and girls who have graduated from school and who now find that the jobs in industry and business for which they spent years in training do not exist. These younger folk, like the adults in the older units, are being made to see this movement not merely as a stop-gap for the period of the depression but as an entirely new way of living. More and more Production Units will be established in the city and at the same time the movement will be extended into the country.

"Superficially the Production Units are much like other groups in which the unemployed are organized for self-help, though the Dayton groups are smaller than most. The unit secures an empty house or store for headquarters, acquires sewing machines, shoe-making machinery, abandoned bakery ovens, and begins to make dresses and shirts, to bake bread, to repair shoes, to cut wood. What the members of the group cannot consume they trade to the city relief stores, to the farmers of the surrounding country, and among themselves for foodstuffs, cloth, raw materials, and other products. The Dayton plan is unlike most self-help schemes in that barter is merely incidental. Within each unit, distribution to the membership is made according to need, each member being required to put in a certain amount of work. Usually the time which the members devote to the unit is greatly in excess of the minimum required. Volunteer work is common and a spirit of comradeship and mutual helpfulness prevails.

"The limitations within which the Production Units operate are obvious. In the city no raw materials can be produced. In order to obtain cloth, raw wool, and groceries which they do not produce, surpluses of clothing and bread and other products must be manufactured. This requires large-scale operations and is dependent upon the unit's ability to secure factory machinery. These large-scale operations thrust upon each organization problems of management actually much more difficult than those in an average factory, because the management has to be democratic. Politics, of course, arise. Revolutions within each unit have taken place, though each has managed ultimately to develop leadership and select a general manager and an executive committee efficient enough to carry on. The larger the units become - that is, the more nearly their operations approach factory proportions - the more difficult become the problems of management and distribution. As long as the units remain in the city and as long as they produce by factory methods surpluses which they can exchange for the commodities they do not make, they will have all the limitations under which cooperative organizations generally labor. Only exceptional leadership will in my opinion enable the units to maintain themselves when opportunities for outside employment increase for the members.

"The Homestead Unit, the new experiment to which Dayton is now committing itself as fast as suitable tracts of land can be secured and the necessary funds raised, goes far beyond the Production Unit. In the Homestead Units, which are to be located within a fifteen-mile radius of the city, the families belonging to each unit will build their own homes and grow their own crops in addition to carrying on the group activities which the unit as a whole may decide on. Each tract will be owned by the unit as a whole; the homesteads will be granted to members under perpetual leaseholds and will consist of about three acres each. The pasture, wood -lot, and community buildings will be owned by the unit and used by the members under rules and regulations established by the whole group. Each family in the unit is expected to build its own home, poultry-house, cow-shed, and workshop; to cultivate a garden, set out an orchard and berry patch, and become as nearly self-sufficient as were the pioneers of a hundred years ago. Trades and crafts will be permitted to develop toward specialization as far as the members desire, but there will be no emphasis on specialization as a good in itself. Large-scale farming operations may be carried on by the group as a unit, just as the city units are now producing clothes, bread, and other goods.

"The plans presented for the first Homestead Unit look toward the building of permanent and beautiful homes. The house walls will probably be made of rammed earth. Cellars and garrets will be avoided and the construction will be along lines developed by Ernest Flagg for beautiful and inexpensive small homes. The homesteaders will commute between the homesteads and their homes in Dayton while building the first wing of their house. As soon as these wings are completed, they will move in and begin to garden, to make their own furniture in their own workshops, to weave cloth on their own looms, and to make their own clothes on their own sewing machines. Electricity will be available not only for light but for power. Machinery will be used to reduce drudgery to a minimum. The crushing tax burden of elaborate water and sewerage systems will be avoided by the use of individual automatic pumps and individual septic tanks.

"Ambitious as this venture may sound from the standpoint of capital required, the financial basis on which the project has been planned by the responsible group of Dayton citizens who are backing it is entirely sound. The funds to purchase the land and to build and equip the homesteads - the labor being supplied by the members of each unit - are to be lent to the units and to the homesteaders for a long term of years on the building-and-loan-association plan. Advances will be made for building material, for machinery, for tools, for livestock, and so on, by a Finance Credit Committee of which General George H. Wood is chairman. Part-time employment and the sale or exchange of any surplus products will enable the homesteaders to repay the loans and keep intact the revolving fund with which additional homesteads may be established.

"One feature of the plan shows the foresight with which the whole project is being launched. In order to prevent the possibility of speculation in land either at present or at some future time, perpetual leaseholds are to be substituted for the usual deeds to land. Thus all the advantages which flow from individual use and individual ownership of the homesteads will be retained, while injustices to the community flowing from the withholding of the land allotted to any homesteader from use will be prevented. The taxes levied upon the whole unit are to be apportioned among the leaseholders in accordance with the value of the piece of land leased to them.

"The outstanding fact about these homesteads is that they are designed not only for family gardening but for family weaving and sewing and family activities in all the crafts which have been neglected for so many years. The loom room and the workshop, with all their opportunities for self-expression and creative education, are once again to become part of the American scene.

They are being brought back to the home in Dayton to fulfil the same functions that they fulfilled in the early American home to furnish economic independence, security, and self-sufficiency. The tools and machines which will be used, however, instead of duplicating, with false romanticism, the clumsy appliances of pioneer days, will be modern and efficient. Power will be used both to eliminate drudgery and to speed up production. Modern inventions will supply comfort. The homestead will furnish the security of which industrialism has deprived us. What I called domestic machinery in my last book, in contrast to factory machinery, is to be given a chance to free the unemployed of Dayton from their dependence upon industry and make possible a higher standard of living than they ever before enjoyed.

Plan for the fifty homestead Units of thirty-five to forty families, each to be established around Dayton, Ohio. The first homestead unit is shown by the star. These drawings were made by Kenneth Butler, Architect, also general manager of the First Homestead Unit.

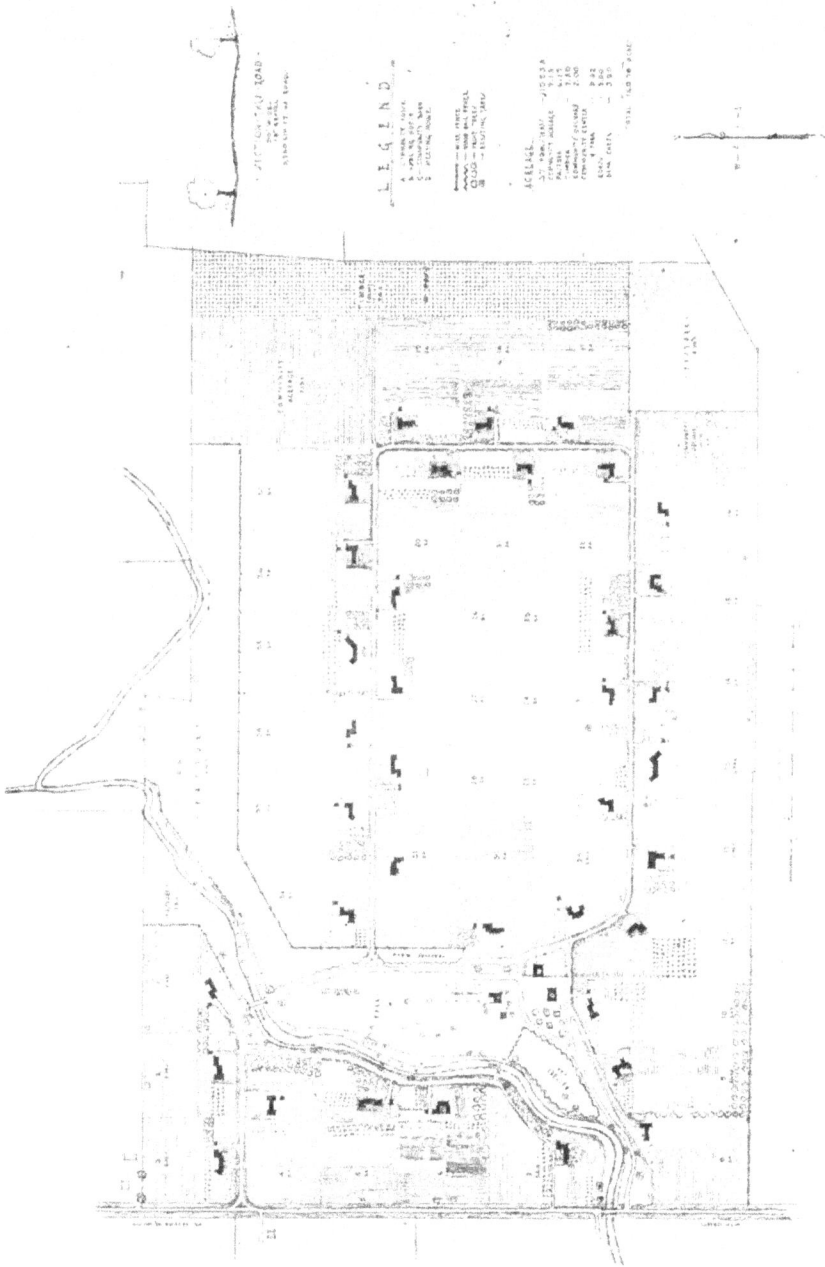

Plan of the First Homestead Unit.

"Dayton is not waiting for economic planning in order to find some way of taming the machine. It is decentralizing production, instead of integrating it; and eliminating distribution costs by making the point of production and the point of consumption one and the same. It is making the home, rather than the factory, the economic center of life, and turning to education, and the artist-teacher rather than to the politician and the technical specialist for a way out. Dayton promises to make social history. Something really new is emerging from its struggle with the problem of relief."

A Birdseye view visualizing one of the Three-acre Homesteads.

Since the above was written, the goal for the coming year in Dayton, provided the necessary capital can be secured, is to establish fifty Homestead Units to enable between 1,750 and 2,000 families to make themselves self-sufficient and secure even under present-day depression conditions. These units will form a ring around the city, as can be seen from one of the drawings reproduced. While an effort will be made to keep the units as close to the city as possible, the tentative limit set by the committee is fifteen miles from the center of the city. Within this limit, the homesteaders will be able to move back and forth between their homes, and work, schools, theaters and stores in the city, with comparative ease.

This expansion of the program for this year is being based mainly upon the co-operation of some of the city's largest industrial and commercial enterprises which will aid in the selection of the families and in spreading work so as to furnish some employment to families which but for homesteading would be forced upon public relief. Some of the families included in the first unit have already been on relief, and will be taken entirely off relief as a result of this cooperation. Living conditions for the homesteading families will be improved at the same time that the burden upon the community for relief is reduced.

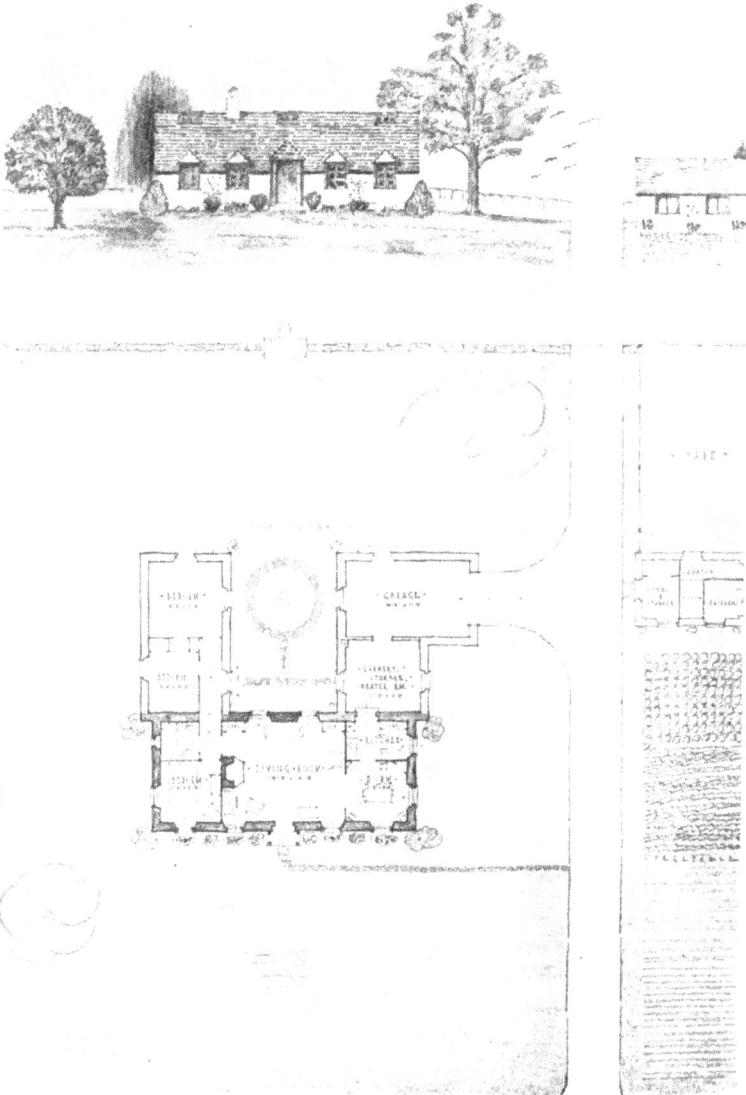

Plan for the home upon which Schedules II and III were based. The section to be built is shown by the shaded walls; the wings were to be added later.

The financial plan upon which the First Homestead Unit is being established, and which will be followed with all subsequent units, begins with a loan by the Unit Committee of the Council of Social Agencies, which is for all practical purposes in this connection a mortgage-loan bank, to the First

Homestead Unit for the purchase of the land and farm buildings, the community machinery and road materials. This loan is to be repaid to the committee over a period of fifteen years. The original farm buildings on each tract purchased, which will usually be farms of about 160 acres each, are to be converted by the homesteaders into community buildings. After the community loan, individual loans are made to each family for the building materials, machinery, livestock and other equipment, and supplies needed for the building of their homes, barns, and workshops, and for the operation of the homesteads. The money for the loans to be made to the First Homestead Unit is being secured locally through the sale of the first issue of a series of Independence Bonds, bearing 4 1 /2 per cent interest and maturing in fifteen years, and secured by all the property of the unit. The capital for the subsequent units is to be secured by the issuance of further series of Independence Bonds, except in so far as government aid makes this unnecessary. Of course, the local situation is such that without government aid the expansion of the homestead movement cannot proceed as rapidly as hoped for. Application has therefore been made for a loan of $2,500,000 from the Federal Emergency Relief Administration and the Reconstruction Finance Corporation for this purpose.

The estimated expenditure for the fifty units, which will homestead between 1,750 and 2,000 families of five persons each, is as follows:

Building materials..$1,175,000.00
Land and community property...510,000.00
Wells, pumps, plumbing fixtures, pipe, electrical supplies...........253,750.00
Sewing-machines, canning appliances looms, and other appliances, and machines for household and craft production...................................148,750.00
Feed and groceries during construction..139, 037.50
Motors, tractors, trucks, agricultural implements, and tools.......108,125.00
Livestock...102,375.00
Seeds, plants, trees...58,292.50
$2,495,330.00

With this development, a new frontier will have been established around Dayton to which the enterprising, industrious, and ambitious families shipwrecked in some way by the depression can migrate, just as in all the great depressions of the past century, they migrated from the industrial East to settle on the old frontier.

Estimated Cost of Establishing the Dayton Homesteads

Schedule of Loans to be Made to the First Homestead Unit of Dayton, Ohio, Inc., and the Members of That Unit

Items	Maximum loan per family	Total loan to unit (35 families)	Period of loan in years	Weekly install- ments[1]
1. Land and community property.	$ 286.42	$10,025.00	15	$1.10[2]
2. Housing materials............	246.25	8,728.50	15	.53
3. Well, pump, etc.............	125.00	4,375.00	15	.29
4. Barn and equipment.........	140.00	4,900.00	15	.33
5. Agricultural implements and tools....................	17.50	612.50	3	.17
6. Domestic machinery and equip- ment....................	85.00	2,975.00	3	.64
7. Livestock...................	58.50	2,047.50	2	.68
8. Seeds, plants, trees..........	33.31	1,165.85	1	.73
9. Groceries and feed...........	79.45	2,780.75	1	1.67
	$1,071.43	$37,610.10		$6.14

[1] Time when payment on each loan begins to be adjusted to situation in each family. Installments include interest at 6 per cent and finance fee of $1.60 per year or 5 cents per installment.

[2] Includes all carrying costs on community property listed in Schedule I.

SCHEDULE I
Loan to Unit for the Purchase of Land and Community Property

Items		Costs
160 acres land, farmhouse, 3 barns, silo, etc.....................		$ 8,000.00
Repairs to community bldgs., wells, etc.......................		400.00
Road-building materials...		1,000.00
Community tractor, plow, harrows, etc., second hand..........		300.00
Community building-machinery		
Concrete mixer..................................	$ 50.00	
Band saw, joiner, circular saws, etc..................	225.00	
Builder's forms....................................	50.00	325.00
Total community investment for each of thirty-five homesteads...		$10,025.00
Investment per homestead.....................................		286.42

Carrying Costs of Community Property:

Interest and amortization of above loan for fifteen years.........		$ 1,021.75
Insurance..		125.00
Taxes..		250.00
Depreciation and machinery replacements......................		235.00
Fencing and sundry expenses.................................		300.00
Total annual carrying costs thirty-five homesteads..........		$ 1,931.75
Average total annual carrying cost per homestead...........		55.20
Average monthly tax or rent to be charged each homestead..		4.60

NOTE: The tax on the various plots are adjusted in accordance with the desir-ability of each plot, and this tax is to be revised annually by the Board of Directors of the Unit acting as appraisers.

Loan to Homesteaders for Building Material to Construct First Section of Suggested Residence, 37½′ x 15′ Inside Measurements

Items	Totals per family		Totals for one unit of thirty-five families	
	Amount	Costs	Amount	Costs
Earth wall.............	24½ cu. yd.	....	857½ cu. yd.	....
Used brick.............	2,000	$ 10.00	70,000	$ 350.00
Sand..................	7 cu. yd.	5.00	255	175.00
Flue lining.............	20 fr.	5.00	700	175.00
Fire brick..............	64	2.00	2,240	70.00
Cement................	66 sacks	33.00	2,310	1,155.00
Gravel.................	10 cu. yd.	7.00	350	245.00
Tar (water proofing)....	20 gal.	5.00	700	175.00
Lumber................		55.00		1,925.00
Rough hardware and nails...............		4.00		140.00
Finish hardware........		8.00		280.00
All metal material (copper).................		10.00		350.00
Insulation.............		45.00		1,575.00
Electrical work, etc.....		20.00		700.00
Paint..................		6.00		210.00
Roofing...............		15.00		525.00
Total for rammed earth construction		$230.00		$ 8,150.00
For stone and concrete-wall construction add:				
Cement................	27 sacks	$ 13.50	945 sacks	$ 473.50
Sand..................	3 cu. yd.	2.75	104 cu. yd.	105.00
Large stones...........	14½ cu. yd.	....	507½ cu. yd.	....
Hauling stones.........		5.00		175.00
Gravel.................	8 cu. yd.	5.00	280 cu. yd.	175.00
		$ 26.25		$ 928.50
Less brick not needed.		10.00		350.00
Totals added.......		$ 16.25		$ 578.50
		230.00		8,150.00
Totals for stone and concrete wall construction........		$246.25		$ 8,728.50
For brick-wall construction add:				
Used brick.............	14,000	$ 72.00	490,000	$ 2,520.00
Hydrated lime..........	96 sacks	24.00	3,360	840.00
Sand..................	1 cu. yd.	.75	35	26.25
Totals added.......		$ 96.75		$ 3,386.25
		230.00		8,150.00
Totals for brick-wall construction......		$326.75		$11,536.25

Loan to Homesteaders for Well, Pump, Plumbing, Septic Tank

Items	Costs
Well	
Drilling well—galv. casing 4¼", 50 ft. @ 75¢	$ 37.50
Sucker rod ⅜"	2.50
Suction pipe 1¼"	5.00
Brass cylinder 1½" x 3½" x 10	5.00
Pump	10.00
Plumbing	
Septic tank	10.00
Drainage pipes @ 4¢ per ft. 8 x 50 x 4¢, 50 ft. per person	16.00
Piping	10.00
Fixtures:	
lavatory 7	
toilet 10	
shower 3	20.00
Water heater	9.00
Totals	$125.00

SCHEDULE IV

Loan to Homesteaders for Materials for Barn and Equipment for Live Stock

Items	Totals per family	Totals for unit
Lumber for barn, chicken-house, and goat-pens	$ 75.00	$2,625.00
Lumber for hog-pen	5.00	175.00
Fencing	50.00	1,750.00
Feeding equipment	5.00	175.00
Bee hives	5.00	175.00
Totals	$140.00	$4,900.00

SCHEDULE V

Loan to Homesteaders for Agricultural Implements and Tools

Items	Costs
Wheel hoe, attachments and planter	$12.50
Spade, hoe, and tools	5.00
Total	$17.50

SCHEDULE VI

Loan to Homesteaders for Domestic Machinery and Equipment

Items	Costs
Pressure cooker or can-sealer	$10.00
500 jars or cans	20.00
Grinder	5.00
Fruit-press	5.00
Sewing-machine (rebuilt)	10.00
Loom, wood-working machine, lathe, or similar equipment	35.00
Total	$85.00

SCHEDULE VII

Loan to Homesteaders for Livestock

Items	Costs
2 goats	$30.00
2 hogs and vaccination	6.00
3 pkgs. bees with queen	10.00
25 pullets	12.50
Total	$58.50

Loan to Homesteaders for Seeds, Plants, Trees and Fertilizer

Items	Costs
Field-crop seed	$ 8.70
Fertilizer	12.61
Vegetable-garden seed	5.00

Trees and plants:

1 plum tree	$ .50	
3 apple trees	1.50	
4 cherry trees	2.00	
5 grapevines	1.00	
30 berry bushes	2.00	7.00

Total	$33.31

Loan to Homesteaders for Food and Feed for Six Months
(Amounts for food are based upon present allowances to families on relief in Dayton)

Items	Amount	Price	Totals per household
GROCERIES FOR SIX MONTHS[1]			
Vegetables and Fruits			
Potatoes	338#	$0.01	$ 3.38
Dried beans and peas	52#	.05	2.60
Tomatoes	130#	.02	2.60
Green vegetables	104#	.08	8.32
Other vegetables	86#	.04	3.44
Other fruits	26#	.03	.78
Meats and Fats			
Butter	13#	.30	3.90
Other fats	78#	.06	4.68
Ham, meat, poultry	52#	.10	5.20
Cheese	13#	.15	1.95
Grain Products			
Bread, flour and cereals	494#	.01¼	6.17
Sweets			
Sugar	78#	.05	3.90
Molasses and syrups	39#	.06½	2.53
STOCK FEED FOR SIX MONTHS			
Corn or equivalent	35 bu.		25.00
Hay	½ ton		5.00
Total			$79.45

[1] *Family Food Budget*, U. S. Department of Labor, Children's Bureau, and U. S. Department of Agriculture, Bureau of Home Economics.

Milk (364 qts.) and eggs (26 doz.) have been eliminated because they would be produced on the homestead as soon as livestock has been purchased.

Extracts from the Constitution of the First Homestead Unit

The preamble to the constitution tentatively adopted states clearly the object of the members of the First Homestead Unit:

We, the undersigned, in order to secure the opportunity to

1. Satisfy our needs and desires directly by production for our own use through intensive husbandry and home craftsmanship,

2. Achieve a permanent basis of economic independence and security,

3. Develop a progressively higher standard of living,

4. Provide for our youth as soon as they are ready, and assure our aged as long as they are able, participation in productive and creative activities,

5. Enrich family and home life by reducing drudgery and releasing creative activity through the use of domestic machinery,

6. Increase control over our own destinies by solving our problems through simple family and neighborhood activities rather than through large, complicated and impersonal civic and industrial relationships, and

7. Furnish to the community of Dayton, which is assisting us to establish ourselves on homesteads, an example of effectual and beautiful living, do associate ourselves together to form a community of homesteads and pledge ourselves to abide by the provisions of this constitution.

The rights of the members to the development of a completely individual life are safeguarded by the following provision:

The rights of the members to absolute freedom in religion, politics, associations, production, and exchange shall never be abridged or impaired by the Unit or its officers, and the only limit to the exercise of the free will of the members shall be the equal rights of all others to their freedom. Any such specific limitation shall be imposed only by an affirmative vote of two-thirds of all members at a special meeting called for that purpose.

The balance between what is communal and what is individual activity is provided for in the following section:

Activities of the unit as a whole shall concern only those affairs which from time to time by vote of the members shall be deemed to serve better their economic or social good than can be achieved by individual activity alone.

In order to prevent speculation in land, possession of the homesteads is based upon a leasehold, the terms of which are made a part of the constitution. The following is the lease agreement:

This agreement made this..............day of A.D. 19...Witnesseth, that..............hereinafter collectively called the lessee, leases or lease jointly from the Board of Directors of the First Homestead Unit of Dayton, Ohio, Inc., the plot of land situated upon its lands in Jefferson Township, Montgomery County, Ohio, which is designated on its official community plan as Homestead Number..........., containing about............square feet, at a rental of $.............until January first, next, and thereafter at such yearly rental, payable in advance on the first day of January, as shall be assessed against it by the Board of Directors of the Unit, subject, however, to appeal to the membership of the Unit within one month at any regular meeting of the Unit; this said assessment to equal as nearly as possible the full annual rental value of the land excluding improvements thereon.

All rentals so collected from the leaseholders shall be expended, first, in the payment of all taxes levied by any authority of Ohio upon the real estate and upon any tangible property located thereon, so that all leaseholders shall be exempt and free of all such taxation; secondly, in the payment of the interest upon the purchase mortgage upon the land; thirdly, in payment on account upon the principal of the purchase price of the land, and fourthly, any funds remaining from such rentals, for such communal purposes as are properly public.

The said lessee may terminate this lease at any time by giving sixty days notice to the Board of Directors of the Unit, and the said Board of Directors, or their agent, may terminate this lease at any time on sixty days notice if lessee shall fail to pay the rent at the time agreed upon, or if the lessee or anyone for whom the lessee is responsible shall make use of the land leased or the communal land in such a way as shall be voted (by two-thirds of the members at a special meeting called for the purpose), injurious to the rights of others.

Upon any termination of this lease except for arrears of rent, the lessee may within thirty days remove or otherwise dispose of such improvements as the lessee has provided, if the land is left in the same condition as when the lease began. If the lessee fails to do so, then the Unit shall dispose of the improvements at public auction, the net proceeds of such sale, less all obligations of the lessee to the Unit, to be turned over to the lessee.

If no such notice be given by the lessee to the Board of Directors, or their agent, this lease shall continue from year to year upon the same terms as above.

All rights and liabilities herein given to or imposed upon either of the parties hereto shall extend to the heirs, executors, successors, administrators and assigns of such party.

In all leases of land, the Unit reserves the right to resume the possession of the land for public or community purposes upon payment of all damages sustained by the lessee to be determined by three appraisers, one to be chosen by the Board of Directors, one by the lessee, and the third by these two.

Nothing herein shall be construed to invalidate the Unit's right to eminent domain.

First Homestead Unit of Dayton, Ohio, Inc.

By_____Lessee.

A "City" of Refuge

(From the editorial in *The Dayton News,* by Walter Locke, vice President of the Unit Committee.)

"There are few cities where the independence of a certain sort of citizen has not been brought into relief by the general difficulties of the depression. In the environs of all cities there is the soil-loving suburbanite. In some cases these are small farmers, market gardeners and poultry raisers who try to make their entire living from their little acres. More often and more successful there is a combination of rural and city industry. Some member of the family, while the others grow their crops, will have a job in town. A little money, where wages are joined to the produce of the soil, goes a long way. Here the whole family has work. The children, almost as soon as they are on their feet, can do productive chores. Incidentally they gain in that process a training and an essential education which city schools with difficulty and only at considerable expense can supply. Here, too, when men grow too old to keep the pace of the shops, there is work to do according to their speed and strength.

"When the depression came most of these members of these suburban families who held jobs in town were cut in wages and hours. In many cases they entirely lost their jobs. What, then, did they do? Did they have to resort to charity? The soil and the industries of their home provided them a job; not a well-paying job, of course, but work and a living, however scant. Except for the comparatively few dollars required for taxes and a few other items they were able, under their own sail, to ride out the storm. The sailing was rough, perhaps; but not to be compared with that in the wreck-strewn town.

"The story of ancient Israel tells how, in the old days of barbarian justice, the "city of refuge" arose. The law of an eye for an eye and a tooth for a tooth was still in vogue; but if an offender against his neighbor could run fast enough to reach certain designated places known as cities of refuge, he could lay claim to his life, at least till his case could be examined on its merits.

"Farming as an exclusive business, a full means of livelihood, has collapsed. Talk of 'back to the farms/ in this meaning, is in view of the condition of the farmers, the sheerest nonsense, almost a crime. Laboring as an exclusive means of livelihood has also collapsed. The city laborer, wholly dependent on a job, is of all men most precariously placed. Who, then, is for the moment safe and secure? The nearest to it is this home and acres-owning family in between, which combines the two. It is the only city of economic refuge anywhere in sight. Till industry and agriculture can both, by a growth in wisdom, be made safe for democracy, this half way place of refuge, the combination of the two gives challenge to our thought."

www.ingramcontent.com/pod-product-compliance
Lightning Source LLC
Chambersburg PA
CBHW022124280326
41933CB00007B/539